LOVE AND CAPES

WAKE UP WHERE YOU ARE

STORY AND ART BY: THOMAS F. ZAHLER

IDW®

INTRODUCTION

It's become a bit of a trend in comics to disavow the idea of alternate universes. Editors and publishers avoided the idea for a good number of years, and only recently have cautiously begun letting the idea back in the doorway, like the bad kid who never wipes his feet on the mat before stepping inside.

I can't help but think that's a terrible loss. Multiverses allow a kind of participation in the reader... we see a glimpse of the familiar, but it's slightly different, slightly askew, and if one is a fan of the medium at all, your heart races a little bit, your imagination starts churning. If this Superman has a mohawk, what does Wonder Woman look like?

It's good fun. Even as a comics writer myself, I like that mental playground.

I sometimes think *Love and Capes* embodies that idea, that it's a book from an alternate universe.

It feels like that, somehow. Like it's a comic whose legacy isn't to be found in the current ultra-violent and often very un-heroic superhero comics of the day. It feels more to me like it comes from a world where Captain Marvel never stopped smiling, where *Sugar And Spike* tops the sales charts every month, and where superheroes acted like people, recognizable human beings.

It feels like in *L&C*'s alternate universe, lovely, graceful art is in high demand, like the art in this book. Where stories are told with mastery of the page, and a genuine delight in the lives of the characters.

I've written my share of hideous sociopaths, I won't deny it. But maybe in an alternate world, my characters could crossover with Thom's and talk about something other than blood and revenge.

On Earth Zahler, stories are told at just the exact pace required, and in the manner that gives the most powerful tug at the heartstrings. A conversation between Mark and Abby about almost nothing is both full of hidden portent and history and delightful as just the joy of seeing a couple in love banter, and have it actually FEEL like the banter of a couple in love.

I like this alternate universe. I like that the vision of one guy has remained so true and so full of clarity of purpose. Thom knows what he wants, he knows the characters, and judging by my reaction to every issue, he knows the audience as well.

I like my visit here every issue. I'm thinking of immigrating, if they'll have me.

Keep building bridges to a better universe, Thom.

Gail Simone is an accomplished comics writer, best known for her work on **Secret Six** *and* **Birds of Prey** *for DC Comics, and* **Deadpool** *for Marvel Comics. She also wrote the "Double Date" episode of* **Justice League Unlimited.**

Once she clears customs, she'll be welcomed to Earth Zahler with open arms.

FOR DWAYNE

YOU MADE ME WANT TO BE A BETTER WRITER.
LET'S SEE IF IT TOOK.

ISBN: 978-1-61377-049-8

15 14 13 12   2 3 4 5

Ted Adams, CEO & Publisher
Greg Goldstein, President & COO
Robbie Robbins, EVP/Sr. Graphic Artist
Chris Ryall, Chief Creative Officer/Editor-in-Chief
Matthew Ruzicka, CPA, Chief Financial Officer
Alan Payne, VP of Sales

Become our fan on Facebook **facebook.com/idwpublishing**
Follow us on Twitter **@idwpublishing**
Check us out on YouTube **youtube.com/idwpublishing**
www.idwpublishing.com

LOVE AND CAPES, VOL. 3: WAKE UP WHERE YOU ARE. JULY 2012. SECOND PRINTING. Love and Capes © 2012 Thomas F. Zahler. © 2012 Idea and Design Works, LLC. IDW Publishing, a division of Idea and Design Works, LLC. Editorial offices: 5080 Santa Fe St., San Diego, CA 92109. Any similarities to persons living or dead are purely coincidental. With the exception of artwork used for review purposes, none of the contents of this publication may be reprinted without the permission of Idea and Design Works, LLC. Printed in Korea.
IDW Publishing does not read or accept unsolicited submissions of ideas, stories, or artwork.

Originally published as LOVE AND CAPES #13 and LOVE AND CAPES: EVER AFTER Issues #1-5.

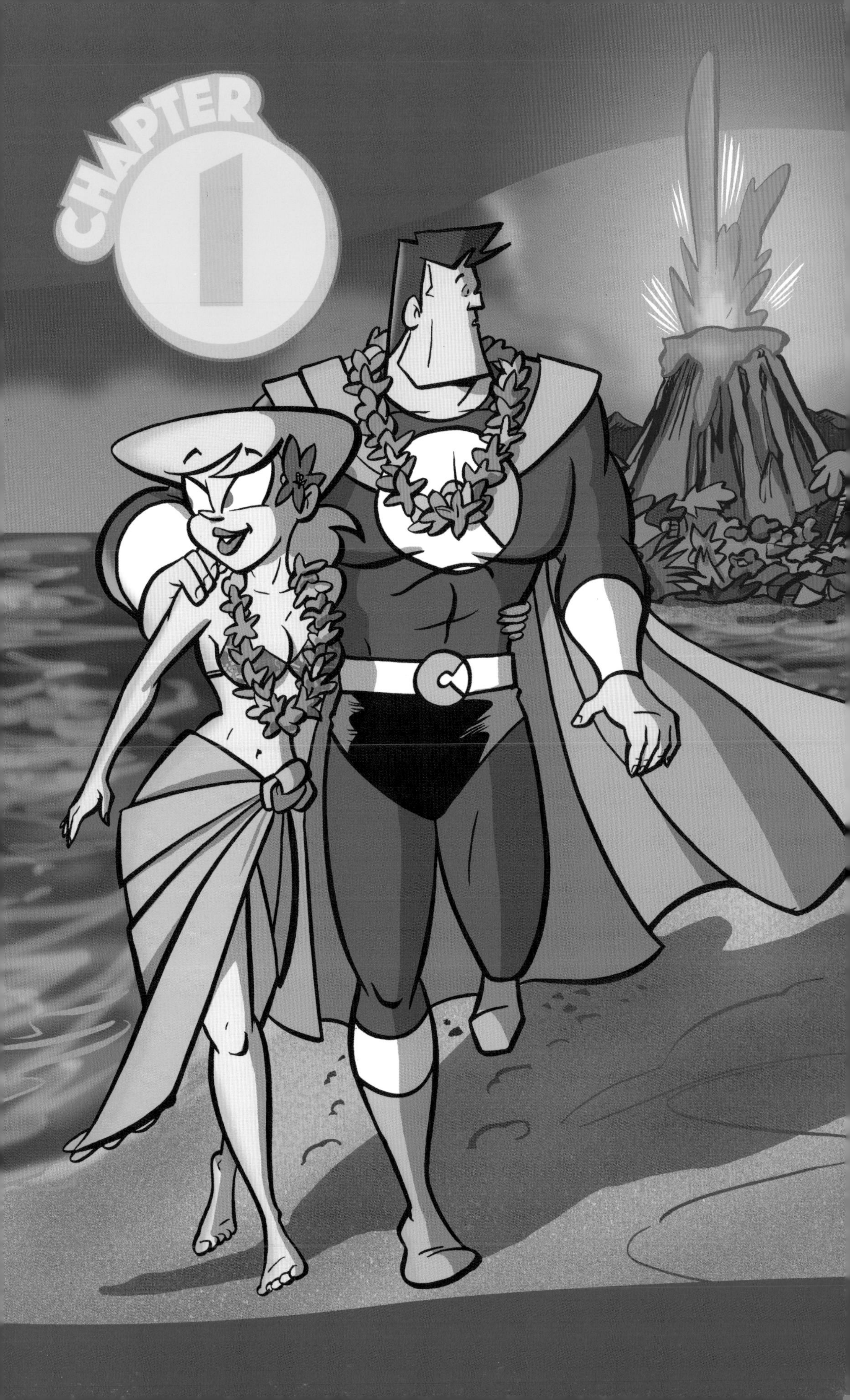
CHAPTER
1

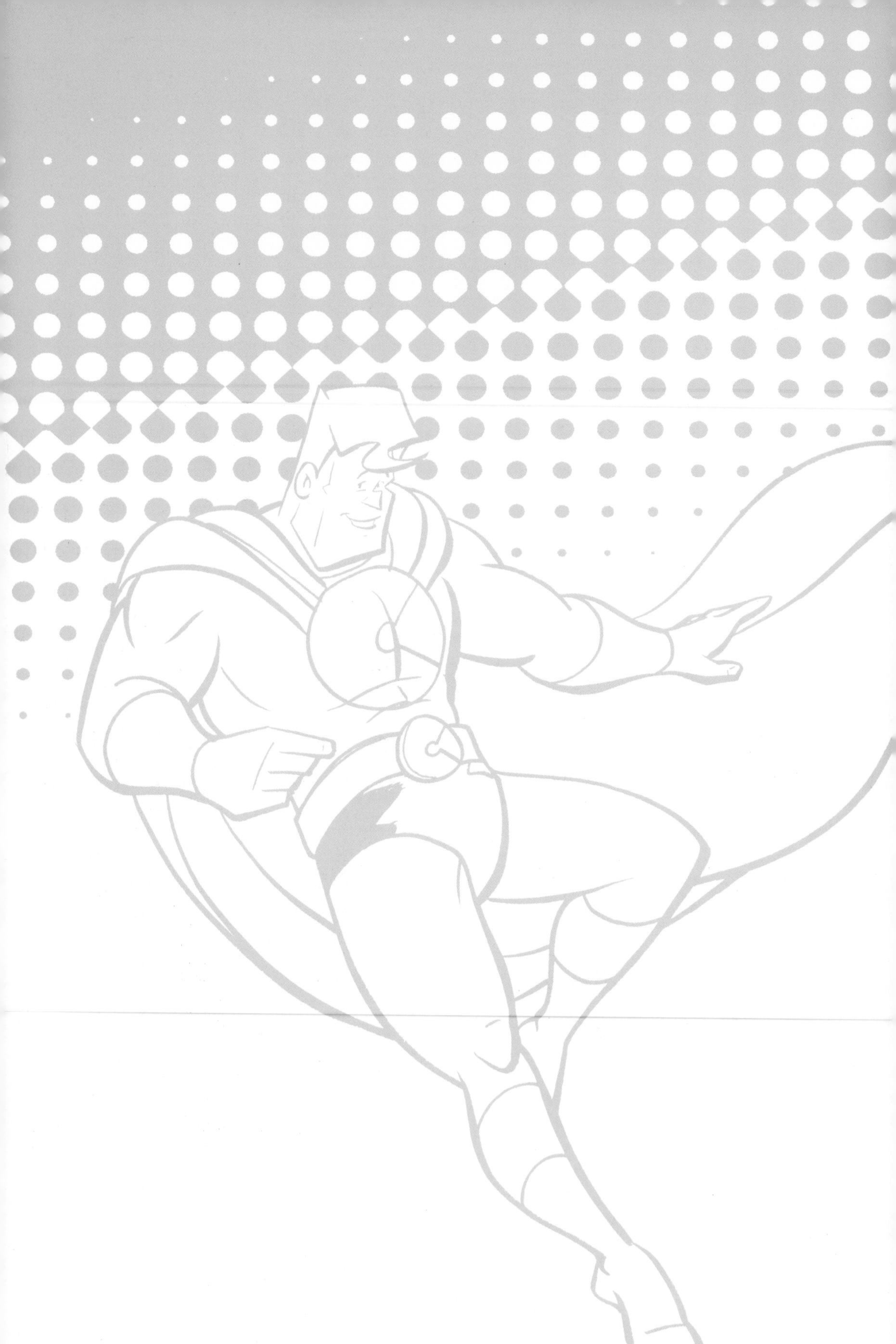

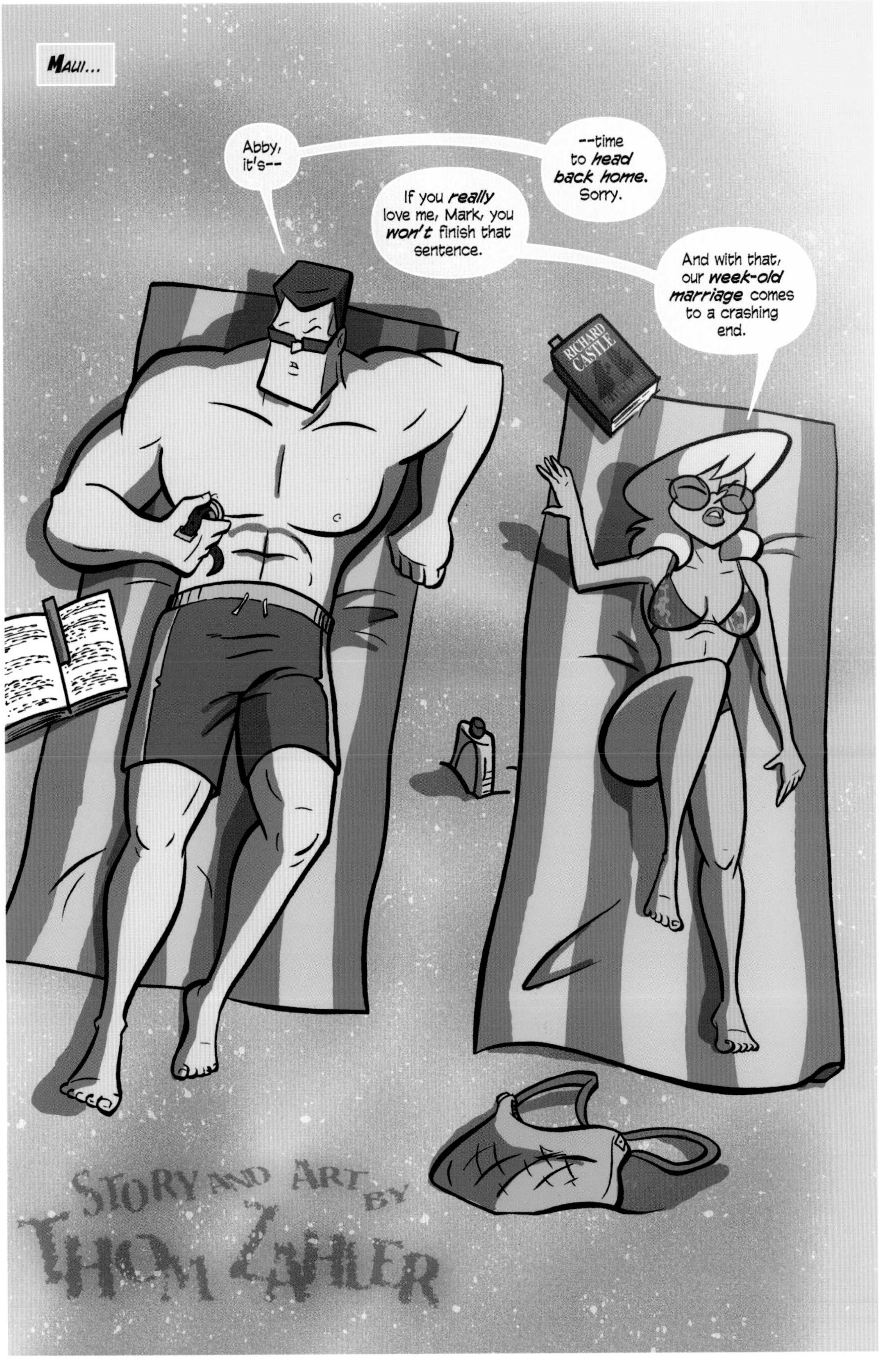

Maui...
Abby, it's--
--time to head back home. Sorry.
If you really love me, Mark, you won't finish that sentence.
And with that, our week-old marriage comes to a crashing end.
RICHARD CASTLE
STORY AND ART BY
THOM ZAHLER

Come on, Abby. We still have to **check out** of the hotel. Let's go.

Nope. Not going. I've decided to stay here.

Really?

Yep. I'm just going to *stay here,* live on the beach. Maybe *solve crimes* and have *adventures* like Magnum, P.I.

You're welcome to stick around, too. I could use a *sidekick.*

Maybe you're *right.* I can do my job from *anywhere.*

See?

And *your sister* can keep running your *bookstore*--

My--?

Time to *go.*

SHORTLY...

All done?

Well done. Now I *match* my Coppertone bride.

LATER...

--c'mon, let me just *fly us* home. I don't want to take a plane again. It's *so booooring.*

Mark, my aunt worked *hard* to get us these tickets. We *have* to use them.

But--

¿Sigh¿ I was going to give you this *on the plane,* but *now's* probably just as good a time as any.

An *e-book reader?*

I saw how bored you were on the way out. So I figured you could use *this* and read at *super speed* and no one could tell.

I even *preloaded* it with a bunch of books for you.

Thanks, honey! Let's see...*The Revenant Road...Heat Wave* and--

--the *Collected Jane Austen? Seriously?*

Time to *expand* your *horizons,* dear.

THEN...

Sir? You've been selected for a *random security screening.*

Lovely.

This is *your* carry on?

Yes, sir.

And it's been in your po--

What's *this?*

Well--

--I'm on my *honeymoon,* you see. And my wife, she--

Stop.

On your way, son.

9

DECO CITY, EIGHT HOURS LATER...

We've begun our final descent into *Deco City Airport.* Currently, the weather is seventy-two degrees.

We know you have your *choice* of air carriers, and we're glad that you chose Oceanic.

Welcome to Deco City.

Excuse me.

Pardon me.

Sorry--

Mark, *slow down.*

--I just didn't want to miss our *connecting flight.*

THEN...

--and we're home.

Hey! That's the *first* time I called your apartment *home!*

It's *our* apartment now, honey.

And I almost forgot-- we have *presents* to open! I wonder what we got?

Blender--

--punch bowl--

--towels, very much *not* from our registry--

--and a salad shooter.

I'm going to go change.

Hey!

No one got us the *gravy boat?*

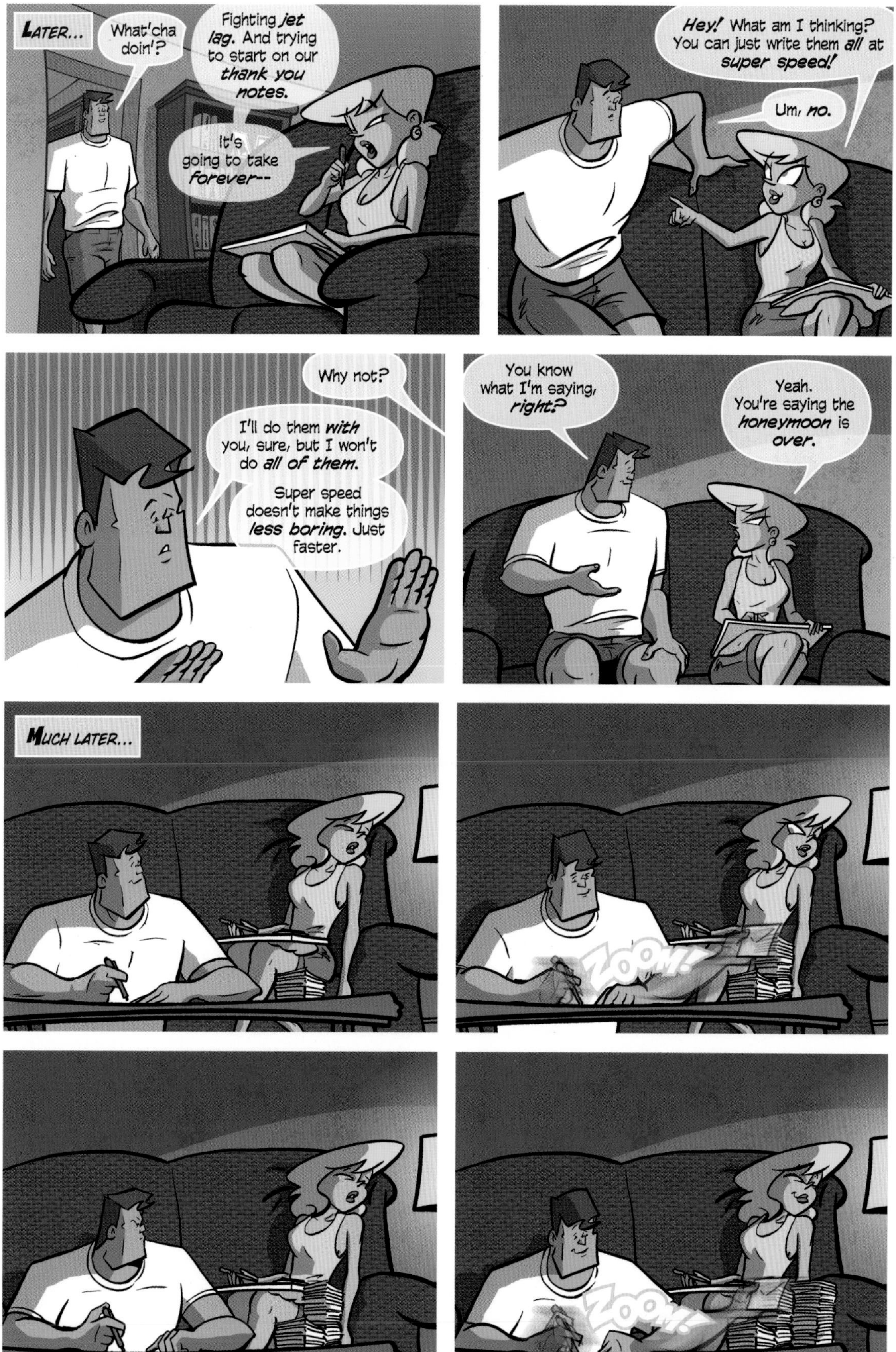
LATER...
What'cha doin'?
Fighting jet lag. And trying to start on our thank you notes.
It's going to take forever--
Hey! What am I thinking? You can just write them all at super speed!
Um, no.
Why not?
I'll do them with you, sure, but I won't do all of them.
Super speed doesn't make things less boring. Just faster.
You know what I'm saying, right?
Yeah. You're saying the honeymoon is over.
MUCH LATER...
ZOOM!
ZOOM!

THE NEXT MORNING...

Good morning, honey! I made breakfast.

I wanted to do something special for our first morning together at home.

I know you're not a morning person, but it's like my Mom always said: "Everyone's a morning person when there's pancakes."

Mark?

Yes--?

Got it.

No talking until after coffee.

COFFEE (AND A SHOWER) LATER...

Sorry about this morning, Mark. It was very sweet of you to make breakfast.

Don't worry about it. Now I know just to make coffee.

Not all of us are as indefatigable as you.

Although, trust me, that is not always a bad thing.

Okay, I'm off to work. What are you going to do today?

I'm going to catch up with all my tax stuff and then head up to the satellite. I'll probably be pretty late.

Me, too. I imagine I'm going to spend the day rebuilding my smouldering husk of a bookstore.

I'm sure Charlotte did fine.

Really? Remind me to tell you the tragic story of Mr. Sprinkles and my trip to summer camp.

THE LIBERTY LEAGUE SATELLITE...

Mermantis, this is *Darkblade*, look sharp--

--tropical storm *Brandon* could turn into a hurricane and cause you some problems in *Atlantis*.

Nah. Not *this* time of year.

Mark! I wasn't expecting you until *later tonight*.

Not as much work piled up at the office as I expected. How did things go *without me?*

No *major* problems. You *realize*, of course, that the world *can* turn *just fine* without you.

Sure, as long as you don't need it to go *backwards* or anything.

Let me go ahead and *notify* the *troops*--

Paul, would you mind if *I* did it?

Not at all.

Liberty League, this is the *Crusader*. I am back *on the board*.

Thank you *one and all* for your *extra work* this past week.

So, how was the *honeymoon?*

It was wonderful! Though if I *never fly commercial* again it'll be too soon.

What have *you* been *doing--?*

Amazonia!

Whoops! Sorry about that, Zoe!

Mark! You're *back!*

Then...

Sorry, Mark, if I would have *known* you'd be here, I would have picked up something for *you*, too.

Oh, *don't worry* about it, I'm fine.

Did you and Abby have a *good time* in Hawaii?

Yeah, for as much as we were *there*.

We kind of used Maui as our *base of operations*, but we just flew to *anywhere* that struck our fancy.

So, one day we had breakfast in *Sydney*, dinner in *New Orleans*, and stargazed at *Machu Picchu*.

We got some *amazing* photos--

--too bad we can *never show them* to anyone.

What about *you* two? Did you have a *good time* at the reception?

Uh, *yeah*. It was--

--*spectacular*.

Exactly.

What? Did *someth*--

WHEEP! WHEEP!

Alert! Possible *dimensional breach* detected.

Sorry, looks like I'm needed *elsewhere*.

I'll catch up with you more *later*.

Well, *that* was *convenient*.

Not exactly.

LATER...

Excuse me, do you have any books on how to build a *happy marriage?*

Abby!

Welcome back! Did you have a good time?

I had a *great* time!

We went, um... went to Molokai and...

Abby?

You're looking for *fire damage,* aren't you?

Maybe just a *little.*

Charlotte, those boxes are *pretty heavy.* They can wait until *Jason* comes in.

Oh, he won't be in for a bit. I gave him the *morning off.*

Really? *Why?*

Because I figured you'd want to gush about your *"super"* honeymoon--

--and it'd be easier for you if you *didn't* have to do it in *code.*

You know, Charlotte, I think I don't give you enough credit for your *managerial skills.*

Surprised how *good* they are?

Surprised you *have* any.

15

THEN...

--how *late* did you stay after *we left?*

Oh, Mark's Mom and I *closed the place down* and then we headed to the hotel bar.

I'm glad you had *fun.*

I did.

I'm just sorry there weren't more *single guys* at the reception..

Yeah. And there was *one less* by the end of the night.

Did you *say something?*

Huh? What? Um, *no.*

I'm not saying *anything.*

LATER...

Wow! Looks like you were *busy* with *special orders* while I was gone.

Big time. I started selling *out-of-print art books* to my classmates in Paris.

But-- I'm don't see where you billed for *international shipping.*

Oh yeah, I *didn't.*

That's how I got them a price they *couldn't* pass up.

Charlotte, shipping to France is going to eat up *all* the profit and *then some!*

Don't worry. I have a *plan.*

Wait--she wants me to *what?*

LATER... Hello, Jason.

Hi, Abby. *Welcome back.*

Thanks.

So, I have to know, how did my sister do as *boss* for a week?

She was *awesome.* Things went *smoothly,* and I don't know that I've had *more fun* working here--

--um, except for when *you're* here, of course.

Glad you still remember who *signs your* checks.

AND THEN... There's *one more* on her pull list. *Gonna Be a Grandma.*

Seriously? Whose order are we filling?

Someone's got a *one-track mind.* This is the *fourth* book on *grandparenting* she's ordered.

I'll bet it's *Mrs. Shaugnessy?* Her *daughter* was pregnant--

Nope.

It's Mom.

So *this* is the way she's gonna play it, eh?

17

THAT NIGHT...

Hello, honey.

Hi, Abby. How was your first day back in command of the *Starship Bookstore?*

Not bad at all.

Charlotte was acting a little *weird,* though. I don't know what that was about.

Really? It's funny you say that--

--Paul was a little *odd* today, too.

Really? They both--

Omigod! I bet they *got back together* at the wedding!

Whoa! Kind of leaping to *tall conclusions* in a *single bound,* aren't you, Abby?

I *don't know* what you mean.

Oh, *this* is gonna end well.

But if *something happened* between Paul and Charlotte at the wedding, *why* wouldn't they tell us?

Abby, I *don't*--

Mark, weddings can make you do *desperate things.* One time, I--

I'm not denying that it *could* have happened, Abby. Just that we have *no idea* if it *did.* So let's *not* get ahead of ourselves.

You're probably *right,* Mark.

Yeah, I think--

Gah!

What?

It's just... being called a *Matron* of Honor will make me sound so old.

‡*Sigh!*‡

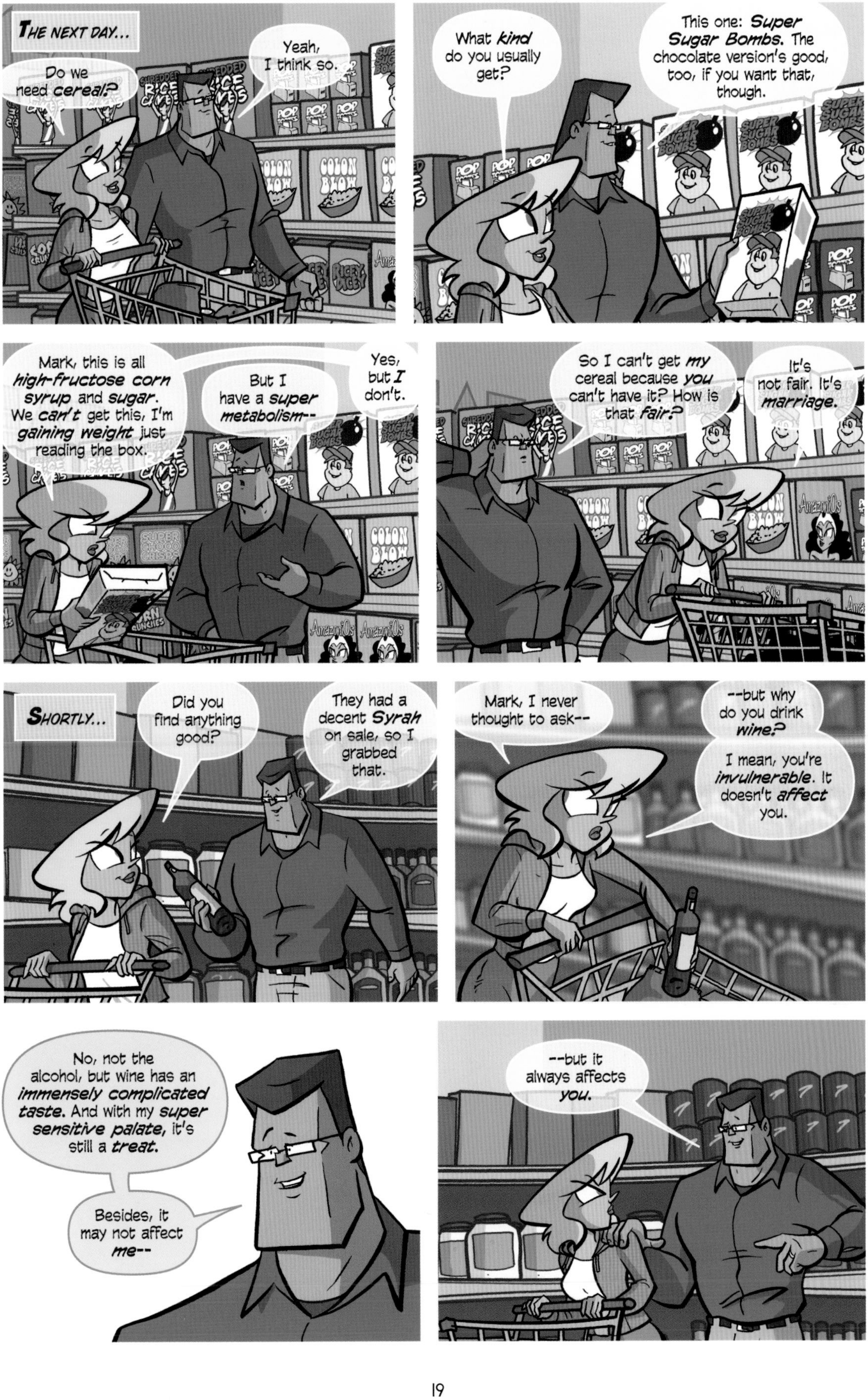
THE NEXT DAY...
Do we need cereal?
Yeah, I think so.
What kind do you usually get?
This one: Super Sugar Bombs. The chocolate version's good, too, if you want that, though.
Mark, this is all high-fructose corn syrup and sugar. We can't get this, I'm gaining weight just reading the box.
But I have a super metabolism--
Yes, but I don't.
So I can't get my cereal because you can't have it? How is that fair?
It's not fair. It's marriage.
SHORTLY...
Did you find anything good?
They had a decent Syrah on sale, so I grabbed that.
Mark, I never thought to ask--
--but why do you drink wine?
I mean, you're invulnerable. It doesn't affect you.
No, not the alcohol, but wine has an immensely complicated taste. And with my super sensitive palate, it's still a treat.
Besides, it may not affect me--
--but it always affects you.

LATER...

I've had just about *enough* of you using Earth as your weapons testing ground, *Animek!*

But your terrain so *diverse!* Where else this one go?

Back to *Planet Prison.* The *Galactic Tribunal* is already sending--

Wait! When Crusader get *married?*

What?

Is being *wedding ring* on your finger, yes?

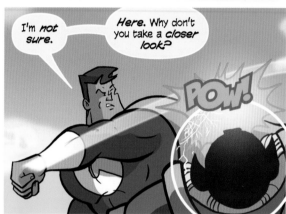

I'm *not* sure.

Here. Why don't you take a *closer look?*

POW!

THAT EVENING...

--so he saw your *wedding ring?*

Yeah. I *completely forgot* to take it off.

I've been *trying* to remember to remove it whenever I change, but it just feels *so right* on my hand that I forget.

At least it was only *Animek.* If the *Evil Brain* had seen it--

Evil Brain? Mark, you're thinking small. It could have been *much worse* than that.

Really?

It could have been TMZ.

≯Shudder!≮

Hey, Mark...

Amazonia and I--

Yes?

Ah--

Um, Amazonia and I used her people's *invisibility technology* so that I could stand with you on the altar.

Yeah, I remember. What's your point?

So *maybe* she could set something up on your *ring* so it could go invisible, too. Then you wouldn't need to worry about taking it off.

That's a *great idea*, Paul! How do you think of these things?

Well, you know, not all of us get to coast on *super muscles* and a *snazzy haircut*.

I think of it as *"rakish."*

LATER, AT AMAZONIA'S PENTHOUSE...

How did it go?

Just *fine*, Mark.

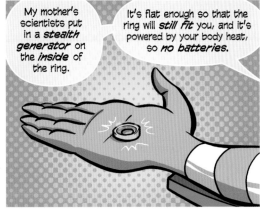

My mother's scientists put in a *stealth generator* on the *inside* of the ring.

It's flat enough so that the ring will *still fit* you, and it's powered by your body heat, so *no batteries.*

Wow! This is amazing.

It's even got a *psychoactive switch.* So, once you *train* it, it'll turn invisible whenever you change from "Mark" to "Crusader."

Come to me my Ring of Invisibility. My *precioussss*--

Ouch! Sometimes I forget that you're a *super geek*, too.

Mark, Mother's scientists wanted me to ask: *what's* your wedding ring *made of?*

They said they'd *never* seen *anything* like it.

I bet they hadn't. Before the wedding, I asked *Elementa* to transmute it into an *Unobtanium-gold alloy* so it'd be as tough as me.

So your ring is indestructible *and* can turn invisible?

Your *ring* has almost as many powers as *you.*

Yeah, well--

--I hear *powered rings* are all the rage with superheroes these days.

Thanks again, Zoe!

BACK AT THEIR APARTMENT...

Hi, honey. Welcome home!

Look, Abby! Zoe rigged up my *ring* so it can turn *invisble!* Isn't it *cool?*

Really?

Your ex-girlfriend made it so that the *symbol* of our *eternal commitment* can *vanish* from your finger and *you* think it's *cool?*

But-- it--

Um...

...but it...

...invisible...

I'm *just teasing.* I *know* you need it to protect your identity.

I think it's great.

Why do you think that's *funny?*

22

LATER...

Finally finished?

Yeah. Quarterly business taxes are *no fun.*

Two hundred employees, *all* with *payroll taxes.*

It's just going to get *worse* if they start taxing their health care plans.

On top of that, he has to *maintain inventory.* Gah!

It's just so *mentally tiring,* you know?

Sometimes I just want a challenge I can *punch--*

∋Snicker!∈

What's *so* funny?

I just find it *amusing* that I married a man who takes *longer* to get ready for bed than *I* do.

3 A.M. OR SO...

Abby? Honey?

You're kind of *hogging* the blankets.

So--?

Excuse me?

What's the *big deal?* You don't get cold. You're *invulnerable,* remember?

YAAAH!

I'm also *super strong,* remember?

THE NEXT DAY...

--it's *simple*. This flips up to reveal the keypad. Just type in *74205*--

--that should be *easy* to remember--

And *why* is that?

It's the *serial number* of the starship *Defiant*.

Well sure.

And then the door slides open to reveal the *secret compartment*. Store *whatever* papers you need in there.

That's not *too* bad.

Just be *sure* to type in the code *right*. If you do it wrong three times in a row, it'll go into *intruder mode*.

Which means--?

Explosive charges will vaporize *everything* inside.

You know, I'm just going to get a *safe deposit box*.

AND THEN...

Um, Abby--?

Yes, dear?

Did you maybe *wash* one of my capes?

You know, I *did*. I was grabbing *laundry* and I thought it was a *towel*.

Why do you ask?

Oh, no reason.

LATER... Mark! Look what came in the *mail!*

What?

This letter... addressed to Abigail *Spencer.*

It's the first letter I've gotten with my *married name.*

It's kind of like in *Miracle on 34th Street* when the Post Office officially recognizes *Mr. Kringle.*

Abby, that's *great--*

--wait a minute!

You mailed this to *yourself.*

Hey, it *still counts!*

AND THEN... So are you two *settling in* okay?

Yeah, I think so.

It's *different* being back home, though. It's not a *vacation* anymore, we're actually *living together.* And for this *only child,* that's a bit of an adjustment.

Well that, and getting used to Deco City again after a week in *Hawaii.*

I still want to take your *mother* there sometime.

I haven't been back since I was *stationed* there. I'll bet it's still a *slice of paradise.*

Oh, it *is.* But I have to say--

--this is pretty great, too.

THE NEXT EVENING...

Just think, Abby, *two more semesters* and you'll be done making this *airport run.*

Oh, it's *worth it.* It's been great working with you at the bookstore again. I've missed all that *talking.*

Although I *was* hoping you would have told me your *big news* by now.

What news?

You know. *You and Paul.* You two got back *together* at the wedding, right?

What? No, Abby, *I'm* not dating Paul--

Really? But--?

--*Amazonia* is.

WHAT?

Well, *you* know how weddings are.

They got together at the wedding?

At the *reception.* Near the end of the night I went to look for Paul--

"--and then I *found him.*"

I wasn't going to say anything until you *called me out.* I figured it was *their* business and *they* should be the ones who told you two.

You *didn't think* I'd want to know about this?

Oh, I *knew* you'd want to know, but I also knew *no good* would come from it.

I mean, *do* you feel good right now?

You *may* have had a point.

26

THEN...

Hi, honey. How was the airport *traffic?*

Not bad. But, Mark--

--well, remember how I thought Charlotte and Paul got back together? It turns out I was only *kind of right.*

It wasn't Paul and Charlotte. It was *Paul* and *Amazonia.*

What? Paul and *Zoe--?*

Yup.

Well, that's-- um... I guess... huh.

I *couldn't* have put it better *myself.*

SHORTLY...

Buy the suit, Barney. Clearly you care about it. Tell the suit how you feel.

Okay! But Ted, remember that was your answer because... the suit is Robin.

I know. Right?

I'm with you, Barney.

Abby, I'm going to go *"get some air,"* if you know what I mean.

Tell Paul I said *"hi."*

CHRONOPOLIS...

You could have *told me*, you know.

Let me guess, *Charlotte* told *Abby* and Abby told *you?*

Your *deductive skills* are as sharp as ever.

So what was the *big secret* for? It's not like I haven't *moved on*.

Perhaps you remember that whole *wedding thing.*

Not to step on your *dramatic point*, but you left your ring on "*invisible.*"

D'oh! Lousy psychoactive switch--

Mark, *I'm sorry.* I *should* have told you sooner.

I *did* try to tell you a couple of times, but I never followed through.

Why is that?

Well, it's *still new*. Actually, *neither* of us have told anyone, because we're still trying to see where it's going.

Plus, while Zoe is certainly her *own woman*, she's still *your* ex-girlfriend.

And dating my best friend's ex *does* fall into a *cloudy* area of *social etiquette.*

I guess it does.

I must admit, though, it's kind of funny to hear a *masked vigilante* talk about following *rules.*

Hey, *laws* are one thing, the *Guy Code* is another.

So *how* did it happen?

You *really* want to know?

Yeah, I *do.*

The past year has been kind of *hard* for Amazonia. She needed someone to *lean on,* and *you* weren't available anymore.

No slight to you there. It's just the way it is.

So she leaned on *me.*

I think it's been building for some time. At the wedding, things just kind of reached a *tipping point.*

In the *coat room.*

Oh, Lord, Charlotte told Abby about *that?*

Women talk, my friend. It's best you learn that *now.*

The thing is, Mark, I think this might be *real.* It's *not* just some wedding-induced fling.

She's *definitely* different than anyone else I've ever dated.

That's for sure.

I'm glad it's out in the open now.

Yeah, *me too.*

And you're *okay* with this?

Okay? Paul, you're dating my ex. It's going to be *seven different kinds of weird.*

But *don't worry,* we'll get through it.

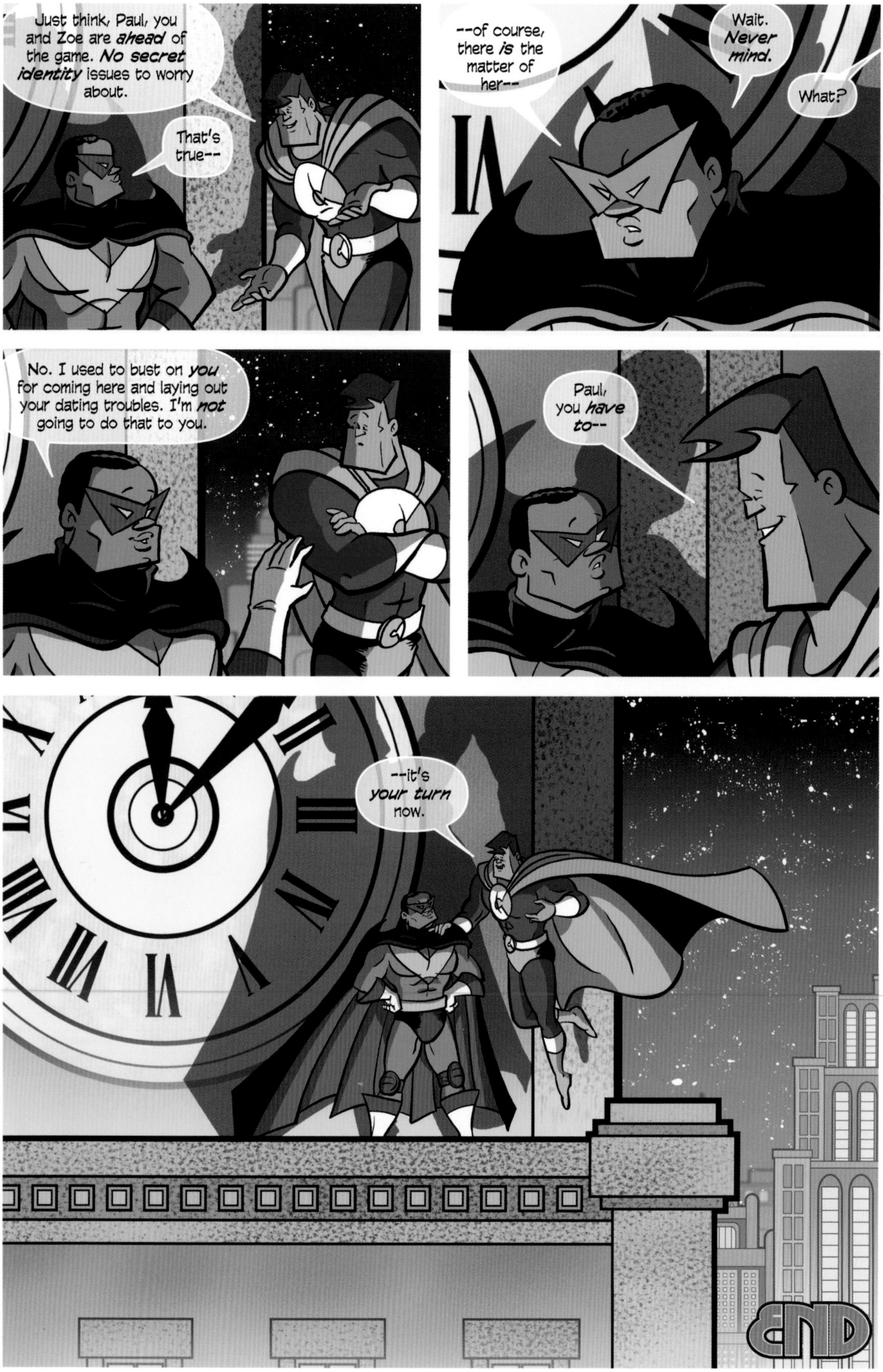
Just think, Paul, you and Zoe are *ahead* of the game. *No secret identity* issues to worry about.
That's true--
--of course, there *is* the matter of her--
Wait. *Never mind.*
What?
No. I used to bust on *you* for coming here and laying out your dating troubles. I'm *not* going to do that to you.
Paul, you *have to*--
--it's *your turn* now.
END

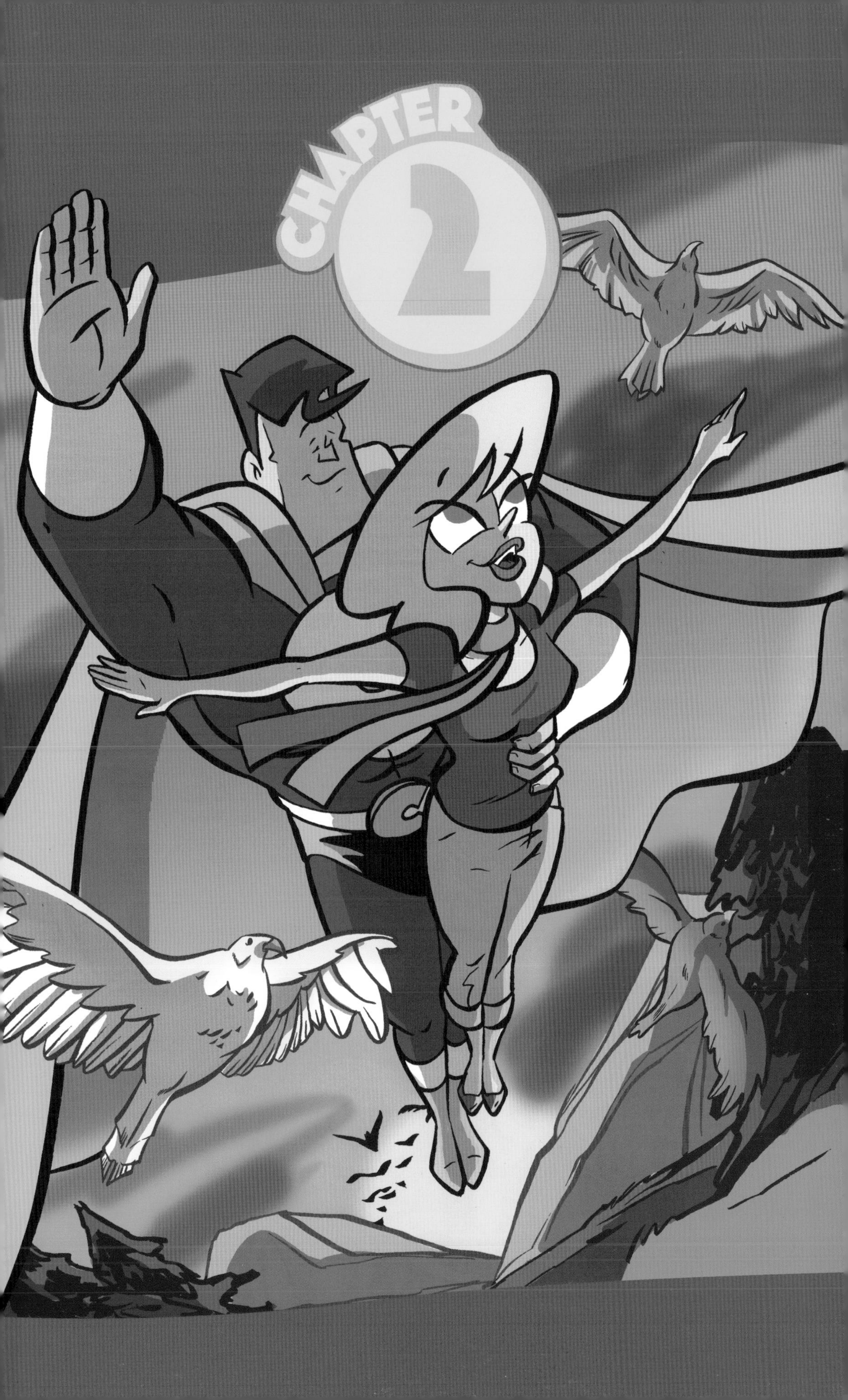
CHAPTER
2

VALENTINE...

YOU'RE OUT OF THIS WORLD!

ZAHLER_10

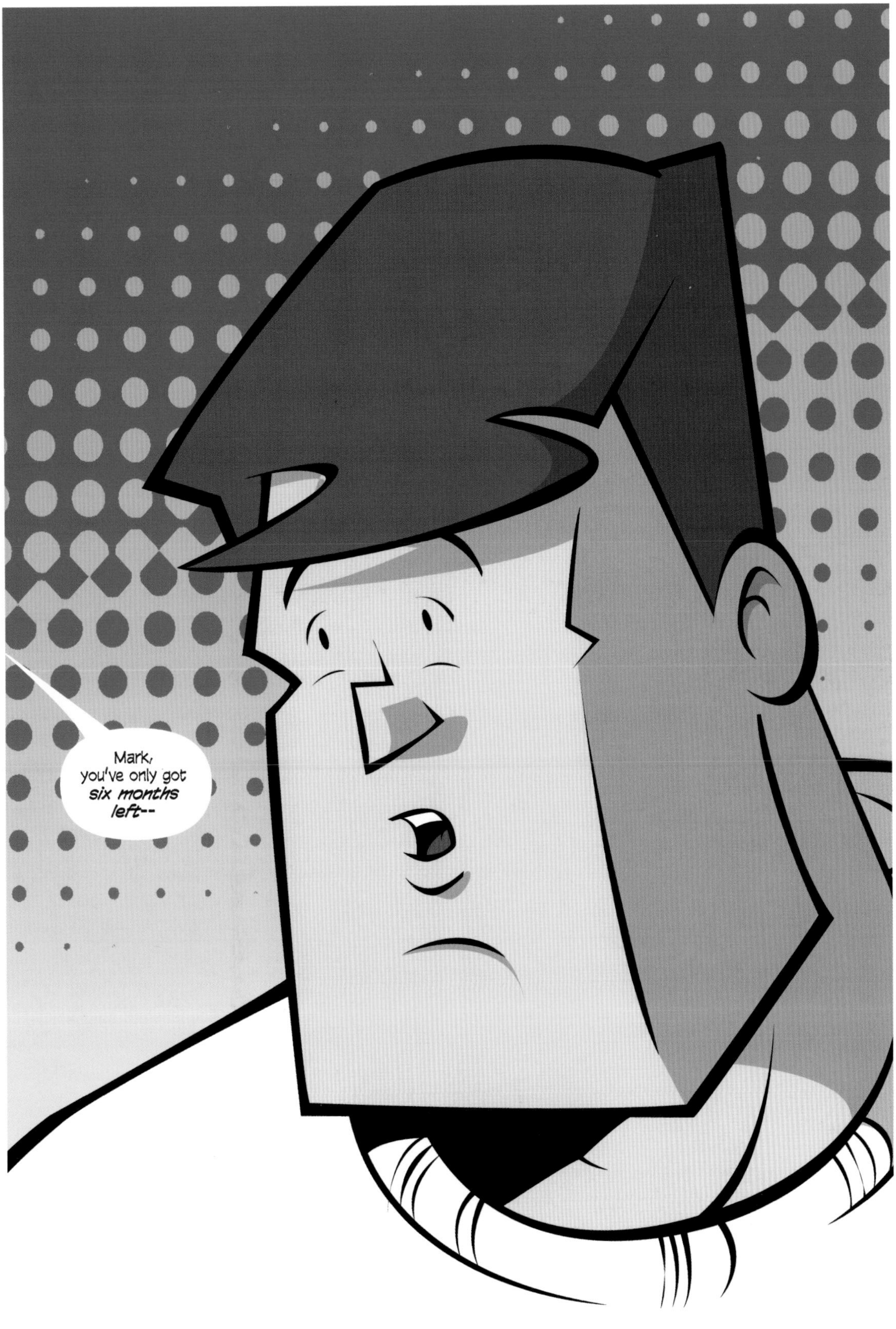
Mark, you've only got *six months* *left*--

--after that, your *lease is up*. We *need* to start looking for a new place.

Can I finish my *cereal* first?

Mark, I'm *serious*.

Here is fine for *now*, but deep down this place is still *your place*. We need a place that's *our* place.

And with *more closet space*.

Abby, *all* I've been doing for the last week is looking at places.

Looking at places the Evil Brain might be hiding does *not* count as apartment hunting.

Unless he's holed up in a two bedroom walk-up with full-size washer and dryer.

Look, I just want to make sure we get the apartment we *want*, not one we have to *settle for*.

You're right.

We'll start looking *this weekend*, okay?

Now, can we talk about *something else?*

Well, we *did* talk about letting my parents in on *your secret*--

Hold that thought. Someone's in *trouble*.

It *doesn't count* if it's *you*, you know.

Hey, you don't get to make *all* the rules.

DARKBLADE'S CLOCKTOWER IN CHRONOPOLIS...

Paul? What's *Darkblade* doing up at this time of day?

Early morning?

Late night.

So what *was* it? Fearleader? Killer Smile?

Amazonia.

Say no more.

Please.

So, what brings you to Chronopolis at this *ungodly hour?*

Oh, Abby and I had a *thing* about finding a *new* place to live, so I was taking a lap around the *planet*.

You *knew* this was coming, though. You talked about it before the wedding.

Yeah, *I know*. I think deep down I was hoping she'd like my place enough that we'd just stay there.

Plus, I don't know if she's ready to go apartment hunting with someone in *our* line of work.

It's not all appliances and exercise rooms, it's *security* and *sight lines* and *power grids*.

Look on the *bright side*, Mark. This will be your big chance to finally get that *skylight* you've always wanted.

Ah, the *city-dwelling superhero's dream*.

So, I take it things are still going *well* with Amazonia?

Oh, *definitely*.

I don't think I ever appreciated *exactly* what you have with Abby and not having to *protect your identity* all the time.

It's nice to be able to be completely *honest* with a woman, you know?

Completely?

Well, *almost*.

I mean, I can't say I told her the *truth* when she suggested we watch *"Titanic."*

What is her *obsession* with that movie anyway?

You know what we should do? The four of us should do something *together*.

Seriously?

You always did get *slap happy* when you didn't get enough sleep.

I'm *serious*, Mark. It's not like we have any *other* couples we can spend time with.

Fine. I'll run it by Abby and see what *she* says.

All right, I'm going to get out of your hair and let you get some *shut-eye*.

And, for the record, I do *not* get slap happy.

Really? Because I'm pretty sure I can find that video of you dancing the *"Blade-tuz!"* on TMZ.

ABBY'S BOOKSTORE...

Lunch is *here*.

Looks like our *postal carrier* made a visit, too.

Of course he did, Jason. A day without *mail* would be a day without *bills*.

Here's your *Zippy Sub*. You might want to eat it slowly, though. It could be your *last one*.

Why do you say *that?*

I was talking to KC over at Zip's and she said that the landlord just *jacked up their rent*.

So our neighbors are either going to move somewhere *cheaper* or *close up shop*.

Say, did *our* rent go up, too?

Saving that sub *won't* be a problem, because I've got a feeling I'm about to *lose my appetite*.

So, how *bad* is it?

Abby?

Um--

--ah--

ARRGH!!

Abby?

Hang on, I'm comi--

BEEP! BEEP!

Abby?

Sorry about that. I'm only in *financial danger*.

SHORTLY...

Jason, is--

Abby's in the *back*, Mark.

Hey, honey. I came as *soon* as I could.

Oh, that's *sweet*, Mark, but you *didn't* have to do that.

Sorry, *rescuing people* is in my *nature*.

Wait, you brought a *truckload of money?*

Um... *no.*

Well then, it's *not* much of a *rescue*, is it?

So what's the *damage?*

Substantial. It'll eat up almost *half* of my profit per year.

And I've only got a *couple of weeks* before I have to sign the *new lease.*

I'm seriously considering *moving* the store, but that would mean shutting down for at least *a month.*

Plus, *this* location works so *well*, I don't want to give it up.

Then *don't.* Go month to month for a while. That'll give you *time* to decide what to do.

It's not like we need *your income* to keep a roof over our heads. I paid for our apartment by myself for *years* and I can do it *again.*

Will *that* work?

Yeah. You know, you're a *great guy* to have around when things get *hairy.*

Well, I *have* been through a *crisis* or two *before.*

CHRONOPOLIS...

F--well, that's *not good*.

Yeah, it's going to put a *serious dent* in our finances.

I mean, we'll be okay, but we've still got *bills* from the *wedding* and it'll mess up our *savings plan.*

So things are going to be *a bit tight* for a while.

By the way, you owe me *five bucks* for the *coffee.*

Hello, boys.

Hi.

Hello, *Zoe.*

Mark, it's *very nice* of you to watch Chronopolis for the night so we can go to this concert. *Thank you.*

Yeah, otherwise, with the *Menagerie a Trois gang* in town, I wouldn't be able to take the *night off.*

No problem.

You covered for me *more* than a *few times,* Paul. I'm glad I finally get to *return the favor.*

Thanks again!

LATER...

This *isn't fair!*

We were *all ready* for *Darkblade!*

Oh, *trust me,* you weren't ready for *him,* either.

MUCH LATER...

You know, *most* women would be upset when their husbands stay out *all night*.

Yeah, but *you're* not *most women*.

You've got *that* right.

NOT MUCH LATER...

Mark? Can you take me to work today?

≶Grumble≶

You know, I don't need *much* sleep, but I do need *some*.

Can't you take the *train*?

Sure. But if I do, I have to start getting ready *now*. If you take me--

--then I've still got *half* an hour.

AND THEN...

You know, I could take you to work *every day*.

Don't forget, I'm meeting with Michael today.

That's your *real estate agent* friend, right?

Yeah. I figured he might have some *advice* for us, both on the apartment and here.

Mark, I *really appreciate* you handling our apartment search while I'm dealing with this.

Especially when I'm sure you'd rather *just stay where we are* for another year.

Yeah, but if we are going to move, we might as well start looking *now* while we have *time*, right?

Definitely. I know I wish I had *more time* here.

Looking at moving *companies* and *permits* and transferring the *phones* is no fun on a good day, and *worse* under the gun.

Well, *don't worry* about *finding movers*--

--I have a lot of *big, strong friends.*

CLEVELAND...

Welcome to *Hillside Realty.*

Hi, I'm here to see *Michael Forrester.*

I'll let him know you're here.

Mark Spencer! What brings you this far east?

Oh, I've got a *real estate question* or two for you.

Sure.

Say, it's a nice day. You want to go *get some air?*

So, *what's up?*

41

--well, I *can't* help Abby with her store space. Commercial real estate is *above* my pay grade.

But your *apartment* is another matter altogether. You *are* talking to an *Accredited Relocation Specialist*.

I can go through the listings in Deco City and find some places that suit those of our *particular demographic*.

I'm guessing something on the *top floor*, facing the lake or other dead space suitable for super speed balcony departures?

Did I *miss* anything?

Two bedrooms. *Lots* of closet space. And Abby would like something close to a Metro station and with an exercise room.

And for the gentleman?

Skylight.

Ah, the *dream*.

I can't interest you in a *house?*

Afraid not. Abby and I love the *city* too much.

Fair enough. Give me a couple of days and I'll pull something together.

So, *how much* am I going to owe you?

What?

After that thing *you* helped me out with last year? It's *on the house*.

Hey, you had Power Glove on the rocks. I just *closed* the deal.

Not that. The thing with the *IRS*.

Oh, yeah. That *was* nasty. We'll call it even then. Thanks, *Windstar*.

Any time, *Crusader*.

THE APARTMENT HUNT BEGINS...

--and this is our *two-bedroom* apartment.

And you said it has a washer *and* dryer?

Right through here.

Um, Abby--

--I think we're *done* here.

≀Shudder!≀ *Roaches?*

All through the walls.

NEXT ATTEMPT...

The closets are *pretty spacious.*

Yeah, it's not bad.

Oh, come on! How do you *not* vote Lucas off? That kid can't sing a lick.

Hmmm... the walls seem pretty *thin* though.

What do *you* think?

I think I'm the *wrong person* to ask.

Can't you hear them--?

Sure. I can hear them talking *about Live Hollywood Superstar--*

--but then again, *I* can hear *Live Hollywood Superstar* from here, too.

So I'm *on my own.*

AND ANOTHER...

Did you *recognize the building* when you got here?

No. *Should* I have?

Hey, *nice* balcony.

Do you ever watch *Channel Seven News?*

All the time. My brother *Quincy* is one of their sports reporters.

Then you've seen it *there.*

You know how they do those *live shots* of the city? They shoot them from *over there.*

Really?

You know you *can't* actually blame Quincy for this.

But it will make me *feel better.*

LATER...

Hey, *Downstairs!* Long time, no see!

Upstairs! You're back in town.

What? Who?

Jason, this is *Yamile.* She's a travel writer for the Deco Gazette. You *might* have met her at the wedding.

She *also* lives in one of the apartments *upstairs.*

Oh. *Got it.* Nice to meet you.

Well, I won't be your upstairs neighbor for *much longer,* I'm afraid.

Don't tell me the landlord raised *your* rent, too.

Yup. You don't know any *good apartments,* do you?

Good? *Yes.*

Good enough? No.

44

CHRONOPOLIS...

Amazonia! I was coming to see--

Paul? Me, too.

He had to go talk to Police Chief Sims. He'll be back *soon*.

You're welcome to wait *with* me.

Oh? Well... *sure*.

So...

Uh, yeah.

He did say he'd be back *soon*, right?

Probably not *soon* enough.

All right, let *me* try to break this tension: Mark, I need to *thank you*.

For *what?*

For being Paul's *confidant* about dating me. I can tell he's been getting some *help*.

Add that to your and my already *complicated history*, and that means there's going to be some *additional distance* between us.

It's not what I'd *prefer*, but I understand it's the way things *need to be* for now.

So, when did *you* get so smart?

I've *always* been smart, Mark. I just haven't always *acted* it.

This thing between Paul and me, it's *real*. And *neither one of us* is good at relationships, so I'm glad he's got a good man like *you* in his corner.

Now, if we could just get you and Abby to *have dinner* with us sometime...

Well, even *I'm* not invulnerable to *flattery*.

Yeah, let's do it.

45

AND THEN... I need you to *beat him up*, Mark.

What? Who?

That lousy money-grubbing *landlord* of mine. He raised my rent *again!*

You can *smack him around* a bit, right? You beat people up for a living.

Honey, I *know* you're upset, but *no*, I can't--

Really? Look at how much he raised the rent *this time*.

Whoa.

Well, maybe just *one* punch.

LATER... I'm going to have to *move* the store. There's *no way* I can afford that rent.

I can't even find an *apartment*, how am I going to find a new *storefront?*

Abby--

I just *can't stop* thinking about it. My brain's trapped in a *loop*.

Apartment... store... apartment... *store*... financial *ruin*... living in a *refrigerator box*.

And just waiting for something *else* to go wrong.

Speaking of which--

--I did tell Zoe and Paul that we'd *have dinner* with them this Saturday.

You *what?*

Hey, at least you're not obsessing about the rent anymore, *right?*

LATER...

--so now I have to go have dinner with Paul and Zoe, *too.*

You've *never been* to Paul's place, have you? It's *great.*

He's got *everything* there. Tennis courts, screening room, *hot tub...*

I am *not* getting in a hot tub with *Amazonia.*

I was trying to think of what to *bring.* Is Paul a *wine drinker?*

Well, he owns his own *private winery,* so I'd say *yes.*

He does? Maybe I'll just bake *brownies* instead.

Good idea. Saturday is the *pastry chef's* night off anyway.

SATURDAY NIGHT...

So *Mrs. O'Lonergan* is Paul's *housekeeper?*

First, *whatever* you do, do *not* call her a housekeeper. *Trust me.*

Second, she's more like a *chief of staff.* Her family has been serving the Darkblades for *centuries* now.

You'll like her a *lot,* though.

Whoa! *That's* Paul's house?

Does it have its own *zip code?*

Two. East wing and west wing.

Mark, how *nice* to see you again. And this must be *Abby.*

I've heard such *lovely things* about you, dear.

Nice to meet you, ma'am.

Come on, I'll show you to Mr. LaCroix--

--and his *trollop.*

47

Oh, Mark, I laid out a *change of clothes* for you in the back bedroom if you'd like.

Thanks, Mrs. O.

Back in a minute.

You had clothes *ready* for him?

Oh, *yes*. Mark's stayed over at the mansion *before*.

Besides, if there's one thing you learn serving the *Lanna Na Hoĭche*, it's to be prepared for *everything*.

Incidentally, you're a *size four*, right?

Size *two*.

Of course. *Whatever* you say, dear.

Mr. LaCroix, your guests are here.

Excellent! Thank you, Mrs. O'Lonergan.

Mark, Abby, We're *glad* you made it.

Thanks for having us, Paul.

I brought *brownies*. I hope you like them.

They're my *favorite*. Thank you, Abby.

Yum!

Zoe, I haven't seen you since the *wedding*, have I?

No, so I hope you brought some *photos* from your *honeymoon*.

I *did*. I loaded some on my *phone* before I came--

Wow. You really *are* trying, aren't you?

Is it *working?*

48

LATER...

So, should we be *worried* about what they're telling each other?

Yes.

Listening in, are we?

More the voice of *experience*.

Although it *is* hard for me to tune out Abby's voice from my *super hearing*.

I'm told a couple of years of *marriage* will fix that, though.

Hey, do the steaks look *done* to you?

Hmmm. Give them another couple of minutes. They haven't *quite* cooked all the way through.

You know, you make a great *meat thermometer*.

That's *nothing*. You should see me julienne fries.

THEN...

You did a *great job* on the steaks, Paul.

Thank you, Abby.

Speaking of *jobs*, Mark was mentioning you've had some problems at *yours...?*

Oh, the *job's* fine. It's the *space* that's killing me.

My landlord's been jacking up *all* the rents in the building.

Mine just went up *again* yesterday.

Has he also been doing a lot of *minor repairs* that he'd put off before?

Yeah. How did you know?

Oh! Is he a *super villian?*

No, but he does have a *master plan*--

--he's trying to *sell your building*.

49

Selling it? I *guess* that explains it. So, is there *anything* I can do?

Not a lot. It's *shady*, but it's *not* illegal--

Wait, she can *certainly* do something--

--she can just *buy the building* herself.

Oh, *sure*. I'll just use the money I get for my next *Maxim* spread. Oh, *wait*, that's *you*--

No, Abby...Zoe's *absolutely right*.

Abby, you're a *well-established* business with a *good track record*. Getting a loan *wouldn't* be as hard as you might think.

Plus, you *might* be able to get a *small-business* or *female-owned*-business grant. I know my foundation gives out *dozens*.

Wait, that'd mean owning the *apartments* above the store, too. We could do *whatever we want* to them.

Buying the building might solve *every-thing*. I think it's a great idea--

--but it's not just *my* decision. Mark, what do *you* think?

Well, I think I'm going to need some *more* wine--

--because it's *bad luck* to toast with an *empty glass*.

All right, Abby, let's buy ourselves a *building*.

LATER...

Shall we adjourn to the *living room*?

Now we could use some--

You're a *wonder*, Mrs. O'Lonergan.

Coffee?

Thank you. But do you have any sug--

It's *already* double-sweet, light cream, dear.

Still keeping *files* on us, are we?

And *look* how useful they are!

Abby, *where* are my manners? I haven't offered to show you around. Would you like a *tour*?

Okay, let me just make sure the *Segways* are *charged*.

I'd *love* one, Paul.

Ha hah.

You know he's *not kidding*, right?

It's a *big house*. In fact, I'm going to grab *another* brownie before--

Really?

Oy! You've had quite enough already!

I'm *not* going to be the first guardian to a *pot-bellied* Darkblade.

SMACK!

How do you *do* that? Sneak up on *me*?

The monks taught *you* some things. The monks taught *me* some things.

51

AND SO...

Whoa. You have your *own* basketball court?

Well, I haven't been able to buy a *team* yet, so it's the next best thing.

I tried out in college, but I was just *too short*. Fortunately, I discovered *sororities* and *keg parties* to drown my sorrows.

I still *play* though. Some of us millionaires have a league. *Mark Cuban* has a great fadeaway jumper, by the way.

I love coming here. It's a great place to *shoot around* and *clear my head*.

Sometimes I think I solve as many crimes *here* as I do on the *street*.

Look at me! I'm a *corporate icon*.

Plus, it gives *Mark* a place where he can make that lame joke. *Every time*.

C'mon, *nothing?* Really?

THEN...

Wait, you're going *public?*

Well, *kind of*. Paul LaCroix is going to start dating *Amazonia* publicly.

We run in enough of the *same circles*, it shouldn't arouse any *suspicion*.

I'm looking forward to it. It'll be *nice* to go out into the *real world* with Zoe.

Plus, I'll get to take her to her first *NBA game*.

And believe me, I am *so* looking forward to it.

Not a big *basketball fan*, Zoe?

Where I come from, sports involve *swords*, *fire*, and the occasional *Bugblatter Beast*.

So, I should take you to a *Detroit* game then.

THEN...

Your library is *amazing*, Paul.

Coming from a *bibliophile* like you, that's quite a compliment.

Oh my God! You have a copy of *"Tamerlane"?*

Abby! Wait!

Yeeeiiii--

You didn't mention you had a *secret* bookcase.

Need I remind you of the definition of *"secret"?*

FINALLY...

Thank you *so much* for coming tonight.

And thank you so much for *having* us. It was *fun.*

We'll have to do this again sometime.

Definitely.

Maybe we can sneak you into *our* place some time.

Hopefully, our *new* place.

Good night.

I have to say, that went *much better* than I thought.

I was kind of expecting a *disaster.*

Well, that's *fair.* When *Paul, Zoe,* and *I* get together, disasters *do* seem to happen.

MONDAY...

I knew he and his wife moved to Tampa, but I *didn't* realize he was *selling the building*, Mrs. Spencer.

It was a surprise to us, too, *Mr. Schaefer.*

Take your time looking around. I'll be in my *workroom.*

Thank you.

Abby, this has definite *potential.*

But, ah, if you *do* buy the building and you need a *maintenance man...*

You and this building go *together*, Mr. Schaefer. I *can't imagine* changing that.

Besides, Mark's *not really* a Mr. Fix-It.

I heard you, and that's *not fair.* I fix *lots* of things.

Yes, and then the *Army Corps of Engineers* fixes them *right.*

Hey, that dam would have held *just fine.*

LATER...

So, what do you think?

It needs some work, but I think we could do it. *You?*

I *really* like it, Mark. It's more apartment than we'd normally be able to afford.

I love the location, *obviously.* It'll be nice to get to work almost as fast as *you* can.

Yeah, I *want* it.

Then let's put an offer in. I'll call Windstar.

I'm just sorry there's *no skylight.* I know how *much* you wanted one.

Abby, we're going to *own* this place--

--we can *put one in.*

LATER...

--so you're going to *buy* the building?

That's the *plan*.

We're meeting with the *bank* tomorrow, and assuming that goes okay, we'll finalize our offer.

Well, I hope it goes through.

Any *big plans* for the building if you get it?

The top apartment needs a *lot* of work, that's for sure. But it's also an opportunity to make it really "*us*."

Other than that, I don't think we want to change too much. We'll *try* to keep all the current tenants.

So *Zippy Sub*--?

They were my *first call*.

AND...

Abby, there's a *Grace* on the phone for you.

Thanks, Jason.

Hello, this is *Abby*.

Oh, sure Grace, I *remember* you. Mark and I--

What? *Ten minutes?* Where? Yeah, I guess so.

Jason, would you pull the rest of Ms. Sharpe's order, and then go ahead and *lock up*.

Sure. Is everything *okay?*

Everything's *fine*. I just have to go meet with someone *upstairs*.

Well, this is *new*.

So, to *what* do I owe the pleasure?

Well, it's-- um, I needed to *ask* you something.

Sure. What's on your mind?

Saturday night... Paul and I--

‡Sigh!‡ I don't know *what* I did, but I think he's upset.

And you're the *only* person I know with a *successful* relationship, so--

--I need *your* advice.

All right, so *something* happened that bothered him?

I don't think it's *huge*, but I can tell it's *something*. I've tried to ask, but you know him... all dark and broody.

Hmmm. Now that I think about it, you did rag on *basketball*.

Oh, please tell me it's not *that*. I *hate* basketball.

Mark's not a *Jimmy Buffett* fan, but he still *goes* to the concerts with me.

Besides, he wasn't *just* talking about basketball. He was talking about the *first time* you'd be out in public *together*.

It was important to him that he get to share that *thing* he *cares about* with the *person* he cares about.

And you kind of just *shut him down.*

Look, you don't have to *like* what *he* likes.

But you can't *hate* it.

56

So, does that *help?*

It does. A *lot.* Thank you.

Well, I won't take up any *more* of your time.

You know, I'm *really* trying to make this relationship with Paul work. And this probably *won't* be the only time I need some *good counsel.*

I know Mark brings Paul *coffee* and, well--

--would you *mind* if I came by with some coffee from time to time?

Coffee? You *do* remember that I kind of *run* a *coffee shop,* right?

Oh, yeah--

But I like *tea,* too.

Then tea it *is.* Thanks again!

Let me know if there's *anything* I can do for *you.*

Well, wearing *pants* would be nice.

END

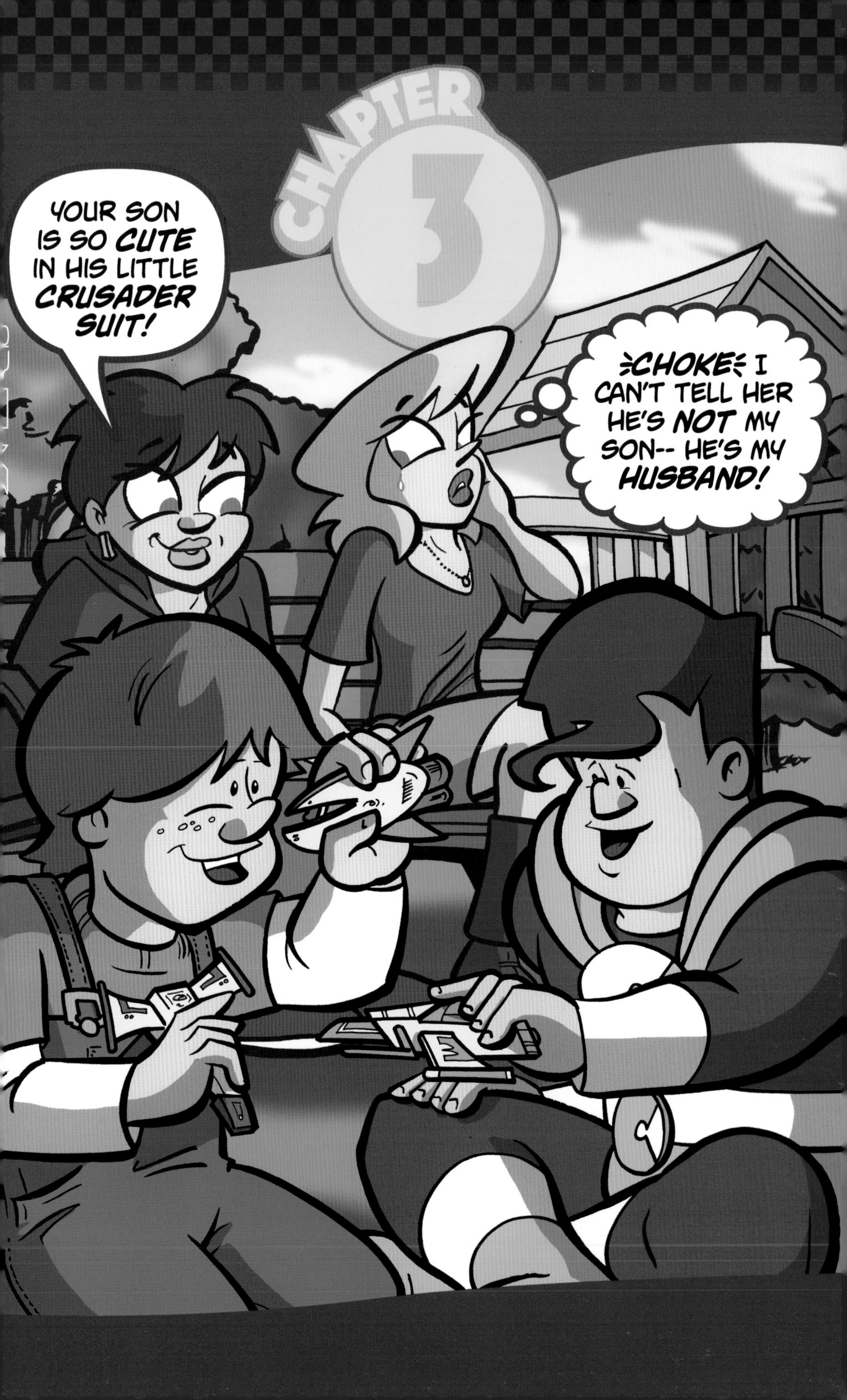
CHAPTER 3
YOUR SON IS SO CUTE IN HIS LITTLE CRUSADER SUIT!
CHOKE I CAN'T TELL HER HE'S NOT MY SON-- HE'S MY HUSBAND!

ALTERNATE COVER BY **TOM BELAND**
COLORS BY THOM ZAHLER

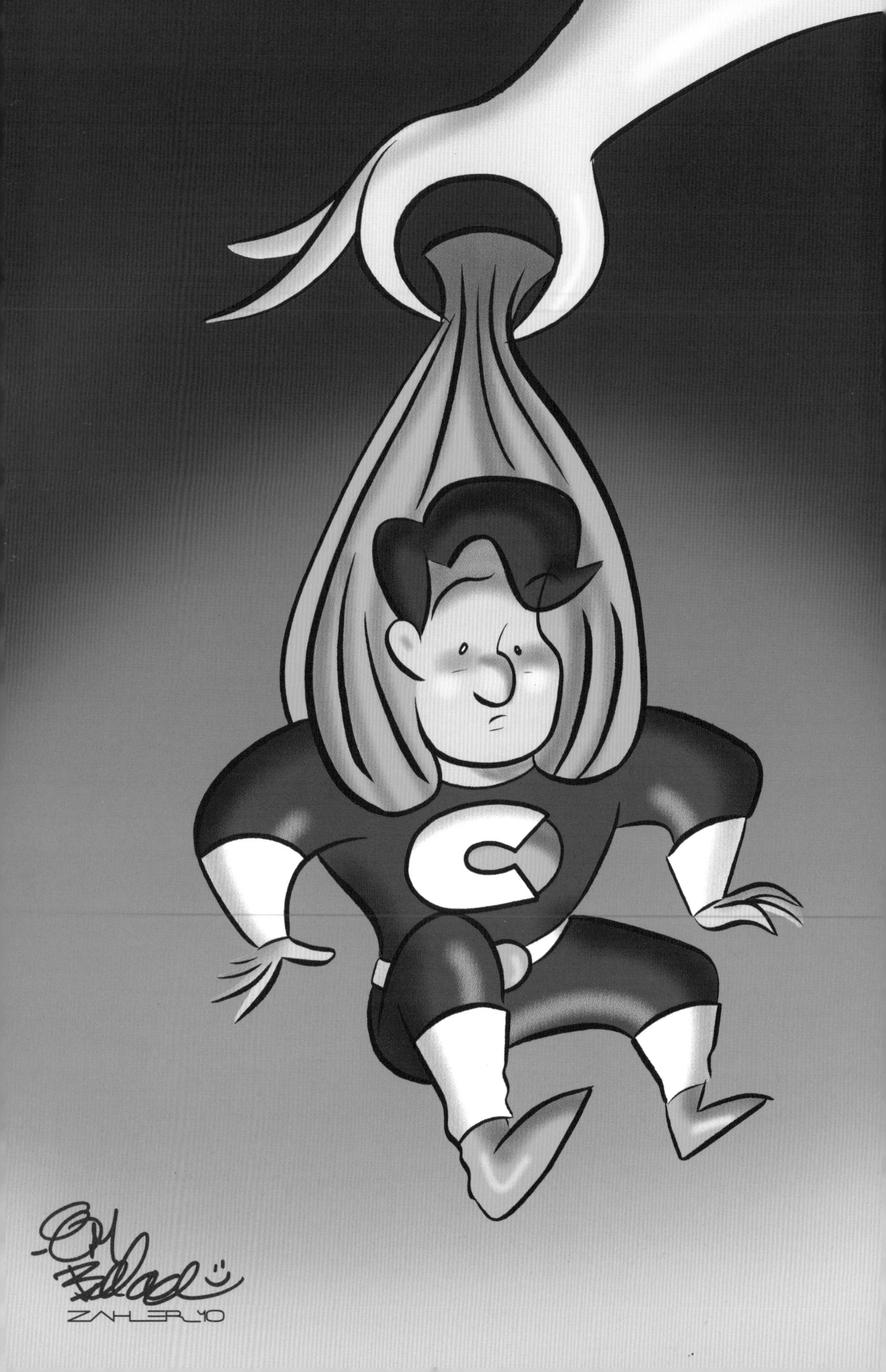

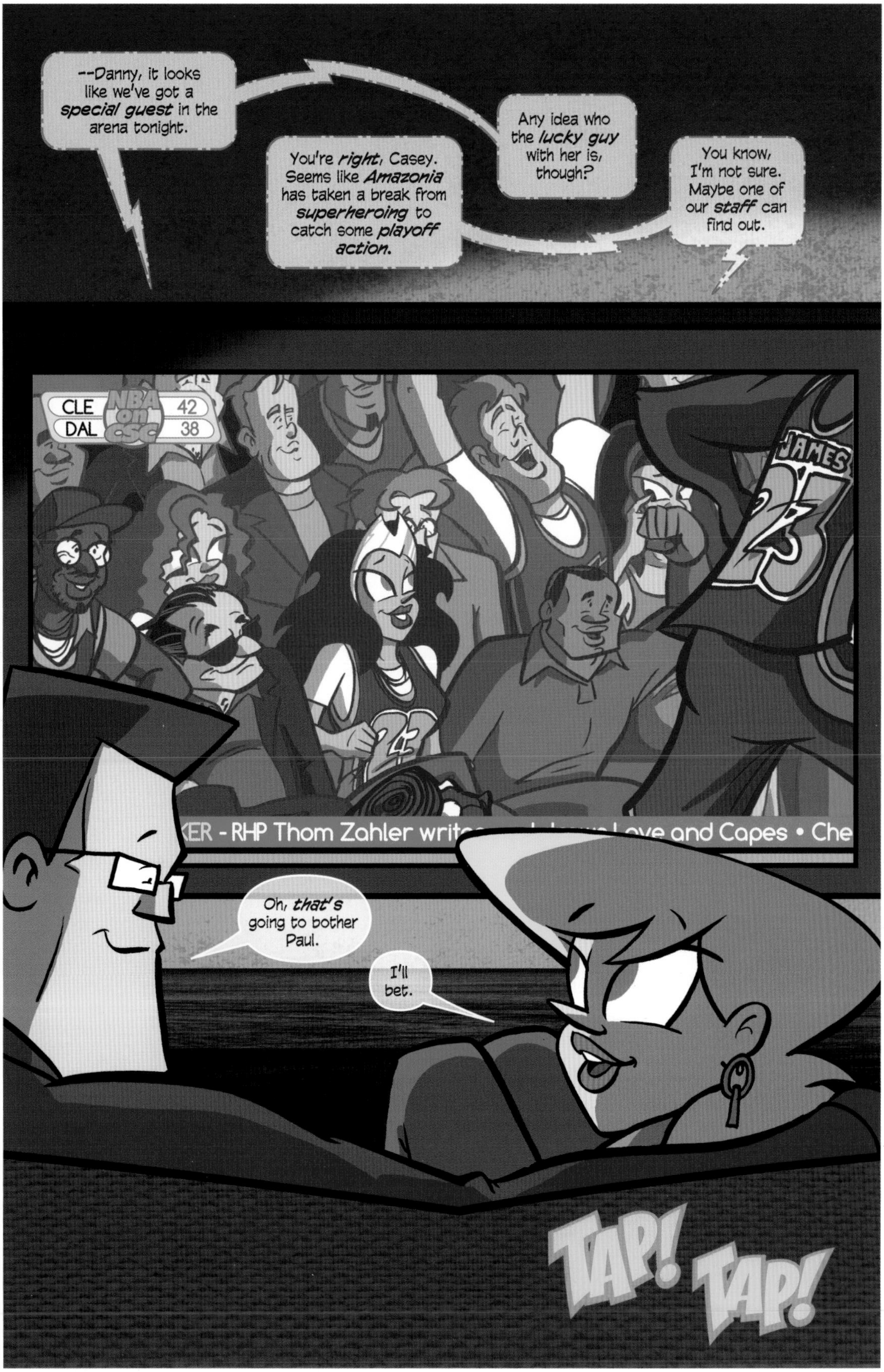
--Danny, it looks like we've got a *special guest* in the arena tonight.
You're *right*, Casey. Seems like *Amazonia* has taken a break from *superheroing* to catch some *playoff action*.
Any idea who the *lucky guy* with her is, though?
You know, I'm not sure. Maybe one of our *staff* can find out.
CLE 42
DAL 38
NBA on CSC
JAMES
KER - RHP Thom Zahler writes ... Love and Capes • Che
Oh, *that's* going to bother Paul.
I'll bet.
TAP! TAP!

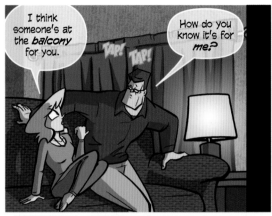

I think someone's at the *balcony* for you.

How do you know it's for *me?*

My friends come to the front *door.*

You may have a *point* there.

Windstar! What brings you to my *window?*

I just brought the *inspection results* from the *building* you're buying.

Whoa! *Our building?*

Excuse me. I thought *your* friends came to the door.

We appreciate you doing this, Windstar.

It's *all good.* I certainly appreciate the referral fee.

So did the *inspection* come back okay?

There are a couple of *minor things.* The owner has *already* agreed to fix them.

I think he's in a hurry to *move South.*

So, once those get taken care of, you're *all set.* Your agent will make an appointment with the title company, and you'll just have to sign.

And sign. And *sign.* And *sign.*

So, it'll be like that *charity autograph thing* we did last year.

Well, except that here every signature will cost *you* money.

THE NEXT DAY...

What do we have *today*? Darjeeling?

Lapsang Souchdong. Hope you like it.

We saw you at the game on TV. It didn't look like you were suffering *too* much.

I'm still *not* a basketball fan, but the live experience was *fun*, I must say.

Good call on wearing a *jersey*, too. Paul *really* appreciated it.

It's a *little* thing, but it goes a *long* way. Helps show that you're interested.

I know Mark liked it when I wore one of those *space cowboy t-shirts* to that movie.

What is a *"Browncoat"* anyway?

No idea.

So what's new on the *big building purchase*?

Are you *excited*?

We sign the papers on *Thursday*. Then we *own* this place.

There's definitely a *joy* to having a place that's yours. The apartment's a blank canvas for us to remodel and, for all the work, that's going to be *fun*.

But we're also going to be *landlords*, and there's new *responsibilities* and *payments* and everything else.

Don't get me wrong, I'm *thrilled* but there's a kind of *shadow* on the experience that's keeping me from blissing out completely.

You know what I mean?

Oh, *sure*--

--Mark's *mother* is coming out to see the place, isn't she?

‡Grumble!‡ She gets here this weekend.

THURSDAY...

Sign *here*.

Initial here.

And *here*.

Congratulations, Mr. and Mrs. Spencer. You now *own a building.*

Thank you.

I don't know about you, but that was just an *insane* amount of paperwork to go through.

Definitely.

After a while, I started getting *paranoid* about the legal stuff. I almost felt like I was signing a *deal with the devil.*

I knew a guy who *did that* once.

At least I *think* so. It was all pretty unclear and *confusing.*

LATER...

That was a *great* idea, Mark.

Thanks.

All right, I think I'm going to *get started* now.

What are you doing?

Mark, your *Mom's* coming here in *three days.*

I don't need her *criticizing* my cleaning skills.

Abby, let's be *honest.* My Mom will criticize you *no matter what* you do.

But if you *leave it alone,* you can at least say that it's *not* dirty because of *you.*

You're a *bad influence,* Mr. Spencer.

You're welcome, Mrs. Spencer.

LATER...

Try all you like, Darkblade. That door is solid *duetronium.*

Crusader?

Sorry. Those Battle Bots were a little more *explodey* than I expected.

It's all right. I could use a little help with this *door,* though.

Hmmmm...

What is it? *Booby trap?*

No, it's just that *color combination--* I think it'd be great for the *new kitchen.*

Just *smash the door,* please!

AFTERWARDS...

Was it just me, or did *Shock Trooper* seem a *little less* afraid of me than normal?

Not that I noticed. Why do you ask?

Now that I'm, well, a little *happier* in my personal life, I'm worried that I might not be projecting my dark avenger of the night vibe as effectively.

I kind of rely on that *grim visage,* you know?

Oh, sure. You need that *fear* and *intimidation factor* to keep people from noticing you don't have any real *powers* or anything, right?

Oh, hey, there's the *grim visage.*

PARIS...

Are Mark's parents staying with *you* guys?

No, Mom and Dad are putting them up at their house. I actually think it was *Dad's* idea.

He loves trading *Navy stories* with Mark's father.

We're all going to go to *dinner* tomorrow and then head to our new place afterwards.

Quincy's even going to make it.

⊰Sigh!⊱

What's *wrong?*

It's just everyone getting together and me over *here*. I wish I could be there, too.

That's *funny,* Charlotte--

--we were thinking the *same thing.*

SHORTLY...

You know, your sister *hates* flying this way.

Well, my sister *doesn't know* what she's missing.

Thanks for coming and getting me, Mark.

It's *no problem,* Charlotte. I'm glad to do it.

That said, you *are* clear on your cover story, right?

Yup, you and Abby flew me over as a surprise using your *frequent flyer miles.*

And I'm staying at *your* place to *keep* the surprise, and because my flight leaves *early* on Sunday and *you're* taking me to the airport.

Really, it's just like being *back in high school.*

Knew a lot of *superheroes* in high school, did we?

No, but I did spend a lot of it *lying* to my parents and staying at someone *else's* house.

66

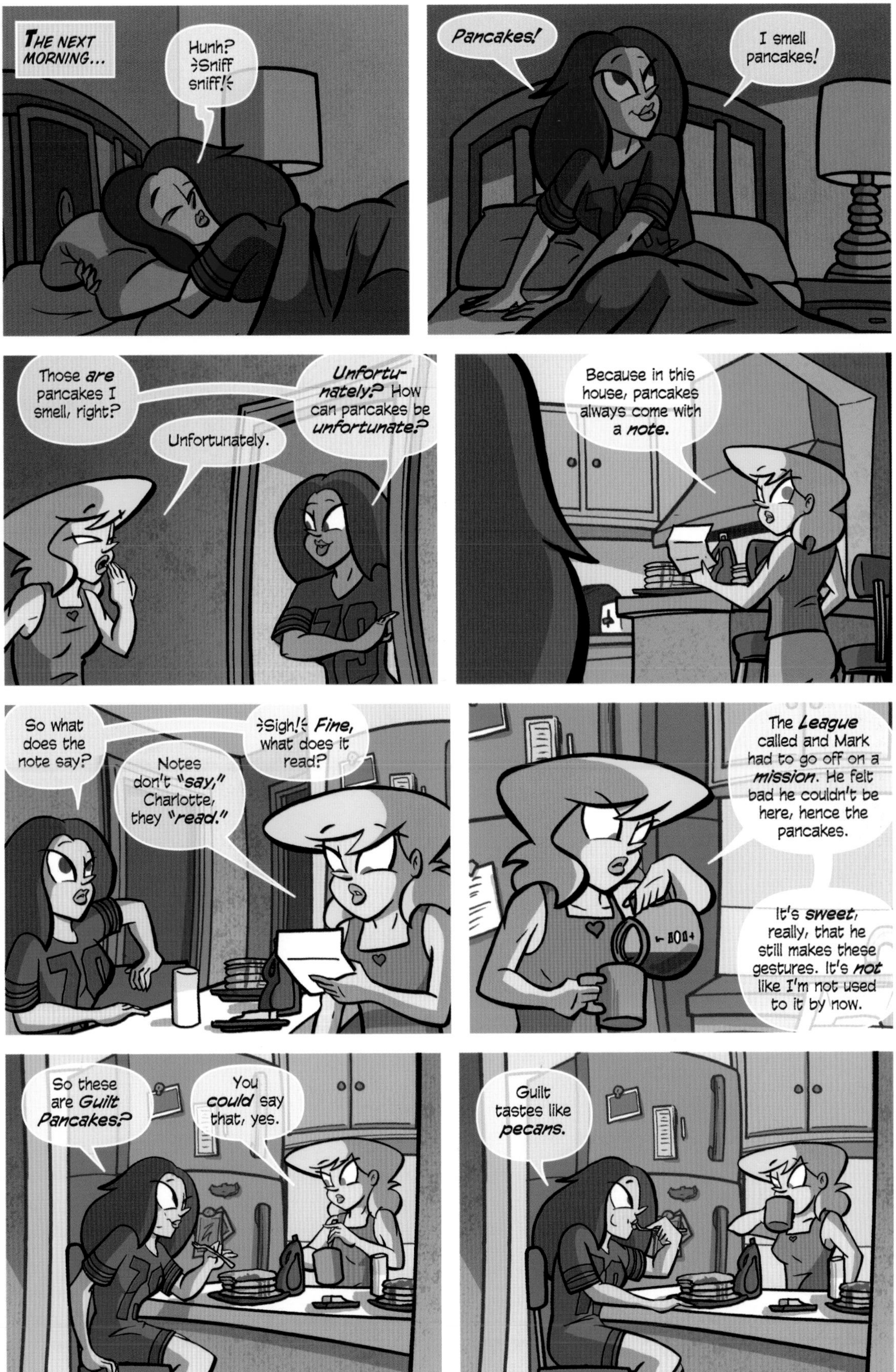
THE NEXT MORNING...
Hunh? ≯Sniff sniff!≮
Pancakes!
I smell pancakes!
Those *are* pancakes I smell, right?
Unfortunately.
Unfortunately? How can pancakes be *unfortunate?*
Because in this house, pancakes always come with a *note.*
So what does the note say?
Notes don't "*say,*" Charlotte, they "*read.*"
≯Sigh!≮ *Fine,* what does it read?
The *League* called and Mark had to go off on a *mission.* He felt bad he couldn't be here, hence the pancakes.
It's *sweet,* really, that he still makes these gestures. It's *not* like I'm not used to it by now.
So these are *Guilt Pancakes?*
You *could* say that, yes.
Guilt tastes like *pecans.*

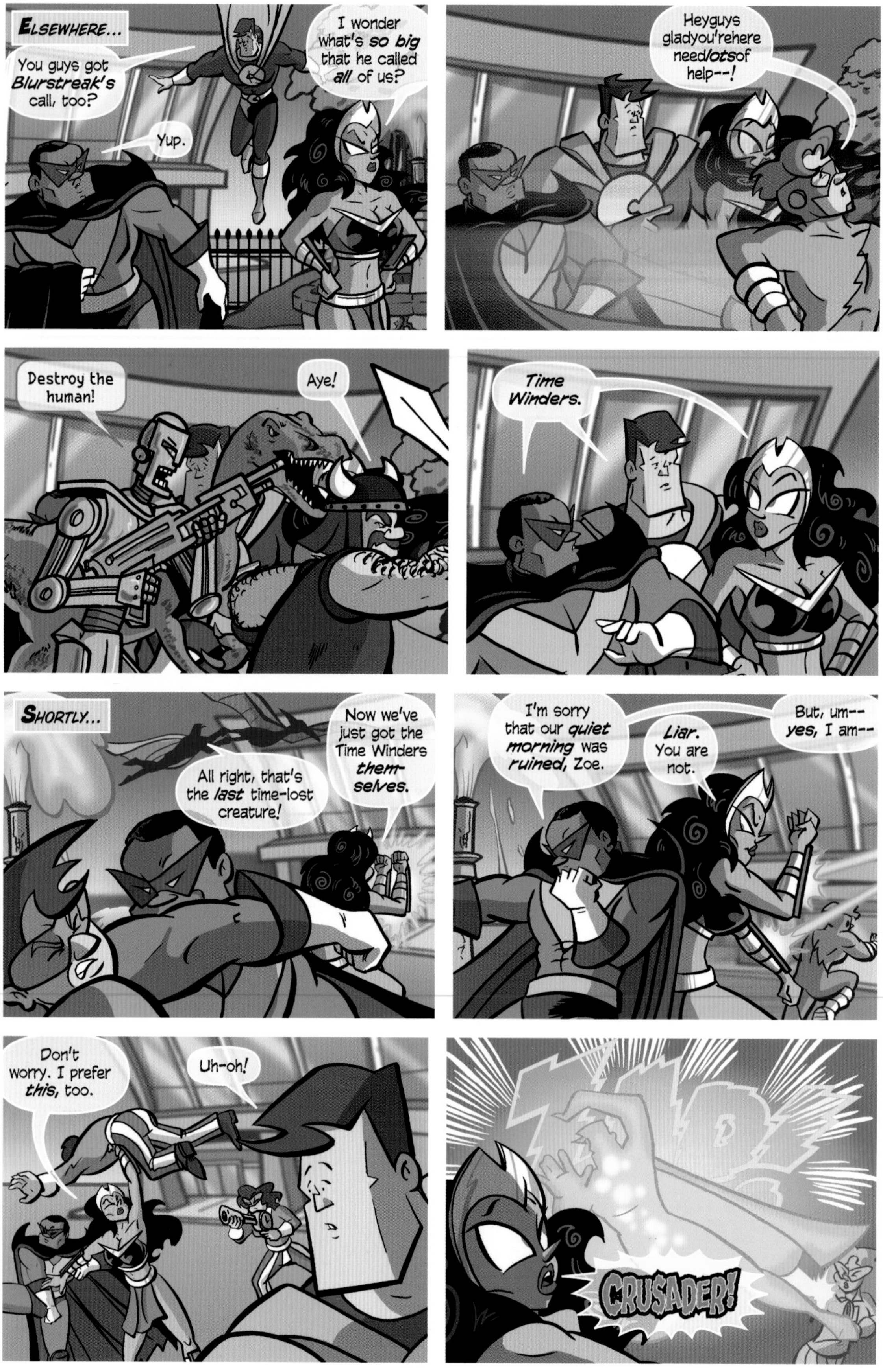

ELSEWHERE...
You guys got Blurstreak's call, too?
Yup.
I wonder what's so big that he called all of us?
Heyguys gladyou'rehere need/lotsof help--!
Destroy the human!
Aye!
Time Winders.
SHORTLY...
All right, that's the last time-lost creature!
Now we've just got the Time Winders them-selves.
I'm sorry that our quiet morning was ruined, Zoe.
Liar. You are not.
But, um-- yes, I am--
Don't worry. I prefer this, too.
Uh-oh!
CRUSADER!

LATER...

THUMP!

Mark?

Charlotte went to visit some *friends*, so she'll meet us at the restaurant.

Our parents will be there around seven, too.

So it's just you and--

Paul? What are *you* doing here? Where's *Mark?*

Abby... there's been an *accident.*

An *accident?*

Oh my God, *what happened* to Mark? Where is he?

Right *here.*

EEEEEEK!

Hi, honey.

THEN...

Paul, *why* is my husband now a *child?*

In fairness, he's *always* been a kid at heart.

Jokes? Seriously?

Sorry.

Mark threw himself in front of a *chronoton blast* from one of the Time Winders to protect Zoe and me.

As a result, he's become *chronologically unstable,* hence the seven-year-old Mark.

Doc Karma checked me out, but he *couldn't* change me back.

He's certain that it's only *temporary.* We just have to *wait* for it to *wear off.*

So, you *won't* have to move to Florida and become a teacher.

You think this is *funny,* too?

That's it, young man, *you're* grounded.

69

All right, I'm going to leave you two to *deal* with this matter. After all, *someone's* got to fight crime tonight.
Thanks for seeing him home, Paul.
This certainly *complicates* tonight, doesn't it?
To say the *least*.
I'll have to tell my family that you're feeling *sick* and *begging off* tonight.
Rats! I really wanted to be there when they saw our new place.
Now, now. *Don't* throw a *temper tantrum*.
Tantrum...? ⸗Sigh!⸗ You know, these *age jokes* are going to get *old*, right?
Not before *you* do.
CHEZ FERRER...
--yes, one of our party *cancelled*.
Hello, dear.
Where's *Mark?*
I'm afraid Mark's feeling a little bit *under the weather*. He won't be here tonight.
Oh, dear.
That's *too bad*.
Abby, ah... exactly *how "sick"* is Mark?
Well, you know how men can be *babies* when they're sick?
Sure.
He's feeling about seven years *better* than that.

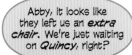
Abby, it looks like they left us an *extra chair*. We're just waiting on *Quincy*, right?

Maybe *not*, Mom--

--look who I found in the lobby.

Charlotte! Oh, my!

Hi, Mom, Dad!

Mark and Abby flew me out here as a *surprise*.

This is *wonderful*. I'm just sorry Mark couldn't make it.

Then you have *nothing* to be *sorry* about.

Mark! I thought you weren't coming.

I thought that, *too*.

Son, Abby said you were... *sick?*

Are you *all right?*

Right *after* Abby left, I started feeling *better*--

--which is *odd*, because usually I only feel better *when she's there*.

Great, now *I'm* gonna be *sick*.

Way *ahead* of you, brother.

THEN...

--Mark, did you know that Miles here has visited *every continent*?

Well, except *Antarctica.*

But, yes, the Navy certainly liked to *move me around.*

Not all of us were lucky enough to be stationed in *Hawaii* like your father.

Hey, Mark, *I* might have to do some traveling soon myself.

And *why* is that, Quincy?

I'm up to replace Dan Rivers as the *color commentator* on the Defenders games *next year.*

If it comes through, I'll be on the move the *whole NFL* season.

Really?

Congratulations, Quincy. That may be the *best* news I've heard *all day.*

LATER...

Oh, *no.*

Mark? What's wrong?

Uh...I think I'm going to be "*sick*" again.

I'd better go. *Excuse me.*

Mark?

Did Mark say he was *sick?*

Sick. *Six.* Same difference.

Yeah, *Doc Karma?* We need to talk.

How may I be of service to you--

A *what?* I suppose 'tis *possible.*

Mine ability to affect and divine the sciences are limited. But you *are* chronologically unstable--

--so exertion such as you describe, the use of your *powers* and the *emotional* expenditures of a family gathering *could* cause you to briefly *relapse.*

You think you could have mentioned that *before?*

Hey, Marky Mark. Are you in here?

Quincy?

Mark? Are you okay? You sound *strange.*

‡Harrumph!‡ No, just still *sick.*

Is there anything I can do?

No, I just need a little *time.*

Like about twenty-five years.

SHORTLY...

Well, I guess *that* settles it.

Text from Mark Spencer
Not getting better. Can you send everyone home?

I'm sorry everyone, but it doesn't look like Mark's getting much better. I'm just going to *take him home.*

Could we reschedule seeing our new place for *tomorrow?*

Of course, dear.

Hang on, Charlotte, I could use some *help.*

Would you bring my car around *after* everyone else leaves? I'm going to get Mark.

Sure.

AND...

God, this is *embarassing.*

Yeah, it's *not* really a thrill for *me,* either.

THEN...

--but it's *not* really my fault, Abby.

No, Mark, it *really is.*

You ruined tonight by *pushing it.* You rushed to dinner not knowing if your situation had settled.

If you'd *waited,* maybe even just met us at the apartment, things *might* have been okay.

I get that tonight was *important* to you, but it was important to *me,* too.

Say, is that a *cop* over there?

Aw, crap.

You've got *that* right.

If you think I'm mad *now,* you do *not* want to see me if I get a *ticket* for not having you in a *car seat.*

74

MUCH LATER THAT NIGHT...

Good news! Three hours and no changes. According to Doc Karma, I'm back to being above drinking age for *good*.

That *is* good news. It's also incredibly *late* news.

Ooops. *Sorry.*

I'm sorry about tonight, too. Sometimes I want the *normal* things in life so much that I kind of lose my footing.

It *also* occured to me how much smoother tonight would have gone if we let your parents in on my *secret*.

What I'm saying is... I think it's *time to tell them*.

Are you *okay* with that?

Okay? Mark, I've been *advocating* that for a while.

I think it's a *wonderful* idea.

Quincy *stays* in the dark, though.

Wouldn't have it any other way.

You know, there *was* something nice about your *second childhood* today, though.

Really?

It was *nice* to see what you were like *way back when*.

You know, you were *really cute* when you were a *kid*.

Hey--!

I'm *still* cute.

You have your *moments*.

MARK AND ABBY'S APARTMENT...

So, this is the place, everyone.

We've got about a *dozen tenants* downstairs, plus the *three businesses*, and then we have the *entire top floor*.

It needs a bit of work, but it's got a *lot* of potential.

Plus it's *really* going to cut down on my commute to work.

Abby, you could just install a *firehouse pole* and get to work even *faster*.

No!

Come on, it would be so cool. It'd be just like *his* place--

Again, *no!*

And...

So, Charlotte, what do you think?

It's pretty *nice*, Mark. I always *wondered* what the top of this place looked like.

Apparently, it's *very pink*.

Yeah, *everything* needs to be repainted. Say, you're an art student--

Art *history* student, Mark. Not that any of my art major friends paint houses either.

Besides, won't you just paint the place at *super speed?*

I tried that once at my parents' house. It *doesn't* work out the way you'd think.

Really? How did it turn out?

Like a giant *Jackson Pollack* painting.

Now *that* I'd like to see.

--and we're going to put in a skylight there--

So, Mom, Dad-- when we get back to Abby's parents' house, we're going to let them in on my *big secret*.

Are you *okay* with that?

It probably *is* about time, Mark. And I think they're perfectly *trustworthy*.

And we can answer their questions from a *parental* point of view, too. That'll *help*.

You guys are pretty close. How do you think they'll *react?*

After the initial shock, I'm *sure* they'll be fine.

As long as they don't *shriek* like a *little girl*.

Hey! He came home *flying*-- carrying you *and* the truck!

Did I ever tell you his voice *actually* went *hypersonic?*

So *that's* why the dog was barking.

THEN...

Mark?

Yes, Mr. Tenn-- um, *Dad?*

I hate to say it, but you have a *problem*.

What the--? It hasn't *rained*, so it can't be the roof leaking.

Unless it's--

Looks like you need a new *water heater*, Mark.

Yeah, I *see* that.

ᔥSigh!ᔥ

Welcome to the joys of *home ownership*, Mark.

All right, Mark, *Quincy* just left, and *Charlotte* went with him--

--so, are you *ready* to do this?

Yeah, I think so. Any *advice* on breaking it to them?

Just one thing, and this is *important*: If they *faint*--

--catch them!

You're just *never* going to drop that, are you?

You mean like *you* did *me*? No.

Hey, Mom, Dad--we're not interrupting anything, are we?

Not at all, dear. What is it?

Mark and I-- we need to *tell* you something.

We've been keeping a *secret* and--

Oh my God! You're **PREGNANT!**

What? No. *No!*

Why would she say that? Do I *look* pregnant?

No, honey, you look *great*.

But I think we need to *refocus* on the narrative here.

Look, Mom, Dad, a couple of years ago Mark told me a *secret*. A *big* one.

He wanted to be *honest* with me, and now it's time to be honest with *you*.

Mark is actually the *Crusader*.

Abby, *please*. If you're going to tell a joke, it has to have some *kernel of truth*.

Mark's *tall*, but he's *certainly* not as tall as the Crusader.

Really?

Oh, my Lord!

Holy--!

I'm *pretty* sure we're the *same height*.

Hi, Mom... Dad.

Abby and I have been discussing telling you for a *while*. We finally felt the time was right.

And even so, it's *not* easy to do.

I'm always worried that keeping this secret from my loved ones comes off as a lack of *trust*. *Please* don't take it that way.

Revealing my identity makes me *very vulnerable*. It's *not* something I do lightly.

In fact, up until a few minutes ago, there were only *six* non-crime fighters on the planet who know what you know now.

So you're in *pretty good company*.

Now, I'm going to guess you have some *questions--?*

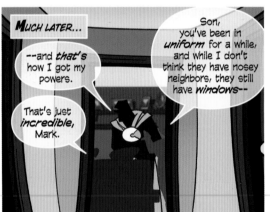

MUCH LATER...

--and *that's* how I got my powers.

That's just *incredible*, Mark.

Son, you've been in *uniform* for a while, and while I don't think they have nosey neighbors, they still have *windows*--

You're right, Mom.

If you'll all *excuse me*, I'm going to slip back into something more *accountantish*.

So, Mom, how are *you* doing with this?

I'm *good*, I think. Just a little *disappointed*.

What? Why?

I'm disappointed I can't tell *Mrs. Yannini* next door.

Then she'd *finally* stop bragging about *her* daughter marrying a *doctor*.

THEN...

I've always thought there's no better way to end the day than with *pie*, JoAnne.

No matter *how* eventful the day has been, right, Catherine?

Mark's revelation *must* have come as *quite* a *surprise* to you.

You know, it's odd... there was a little bit of *shock*, but I wouldn't say "*surprise*."

I guess I always figured that if the Crusader *was* going to be someone else--

--it just *makes sense* he'd be someone like *Mark*.

MEANWHILE...

I have to ask, Jerry, *how* did you do it? How did you raise a boy like Mark?

What do you mean?

Well, I know *Quincy* was *quite* the handful. I can't even imagine raising a son that had *super powers*.

Thankfully, Mark's powers didn't manifest until his *late teens*. That helped.

Oh, good. I'd hate to think you missed out on all those traditional *father-son moments*.

You know, I remember the first time Quincy *actually* beat me in one-on-one, and--

Wait--!

This means Mark *let* me win at tennis last week.

Yeah, you're going to want to stick with *board games* from now on.

Except *Monopoly*. The boy *is* an *accountant*.

AND THEN...

All right, Mom, I think we're going to head *home*.

Okay. You know, *before* you go--

Mark, do you want to take some of that *pie* home with you?

Hmm? Oh, sure. *Please.*

You look like you have *something* on your *mind*, dear.

Yeah, kinda. I know we dropped a bomb on you two, but--

--is it just me, or is Abby's dad treating me kind of-- *coldly?*

It's *not* just you. I noticed it, too.

And I think I know *why.*

Mark, all I wanted for Abby to find in a *husband* was a *good man* who *loved her deeply* and would *take care of her.*

So today, *I* just learned that you were even *more* that man than I thought.

But fathers and daughters have a *different* relationship. Abby's father was the most *important* man in the world to her. I know. I was the *same way* with my father.

So when daughters find a husband, the fathers feel like they're being *replaced.*

Miles has *always* been a little jealous of you, Mark. It's just *natural*. But now he finds out *exactly* who you are, and I'm sure he's asking himself "What does she still need me for *at all?*"

He'll come around, Mark. It'll just take some *time*. And maybe a little special effort on your part.

I never would have thought of that.

But... I think I *might* know a way to make that *special effort.*

THE NEXT DAY...

All right, get *ready*...

...and *there!*

Antarctica! I'm finally setting foot on Antarctica.

My God, it's beautiful.

How did you *know*, Mark? How did you know I *wanted* to come here?

When my Dad mentioned you'd been to every continent, you sounded *disappointed* about skipping *this one*. Didn't seem right for you to not *hit for the cycle*.

I *never* thought I'd make it here.

I'd probably shed a tear if I didn't think that it'd *freeze* to my *face*.

Past that ridge is *McMurdo Station*. I come down and play poker with the guys every now and then.

I'd take you there, but then they'd start asking *questions* and--well, *you understand*, right?

I understand *that*, Mark. What I don't quite understand is how I warranted this special trip.

Well, a *couple* of reasons...

One, you might as well get some *benefits* from knowing me, because my secret and I can be a bit of a *hassle*.

Just in the time that Abby's known, she's gotten *super powers*, dealt with my *evil twin*, went to another dimension and travelled *back in time*--

--all things I should probably have brought up a little more tactfully. *Sorry.*

And *two*, I wanted to ask for your *help*.

My help? What do you need *me* for? You can do *anything*.

That's *not* true--

I can't replace a *water heater*.

What?

I own my *own home* now, and while I've *got* a handyman, I'd like to learn to take care of things *myself*, too.

Super powers help you do a lot of things, but they *don't* tell you how to make major household repairs.

Not the way, say, serving in the *engine room* of a *submarine* does. Abby said that's where you learned how to do things, right?

That's true. And I'd *love* to show you. I always *wanted* to teach Quincy, but he never had much interest.

You want to take care of it *now?*

Sure, if you're ready to *leave*.

Absolutely. Mark, this has been *fantastic*, and I'll always *treasure* the memory--

--but, right now, I'll help you do *anything* that has the word "*heater*" in it.

END

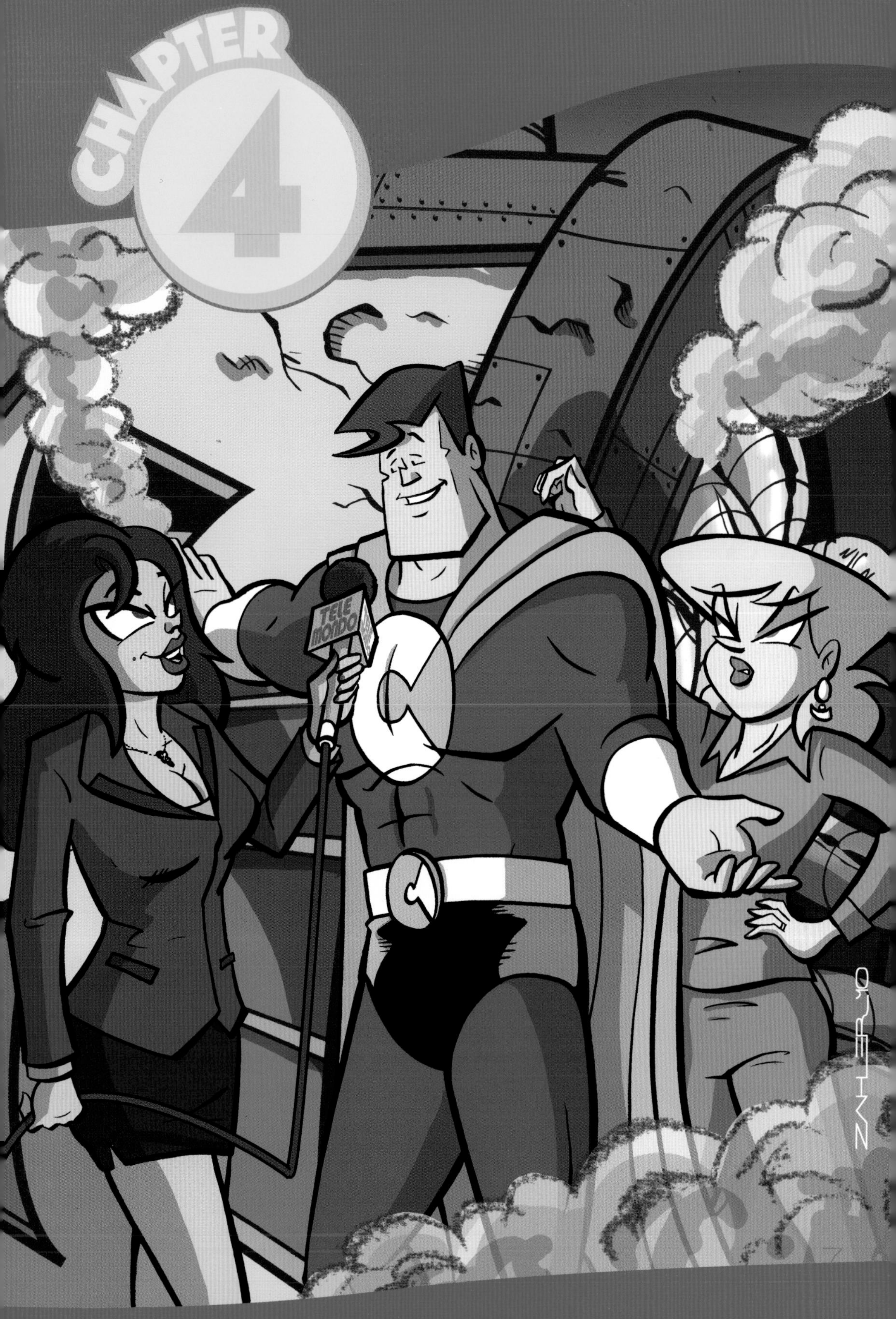
CHAPTER
4
TELE
MONDO

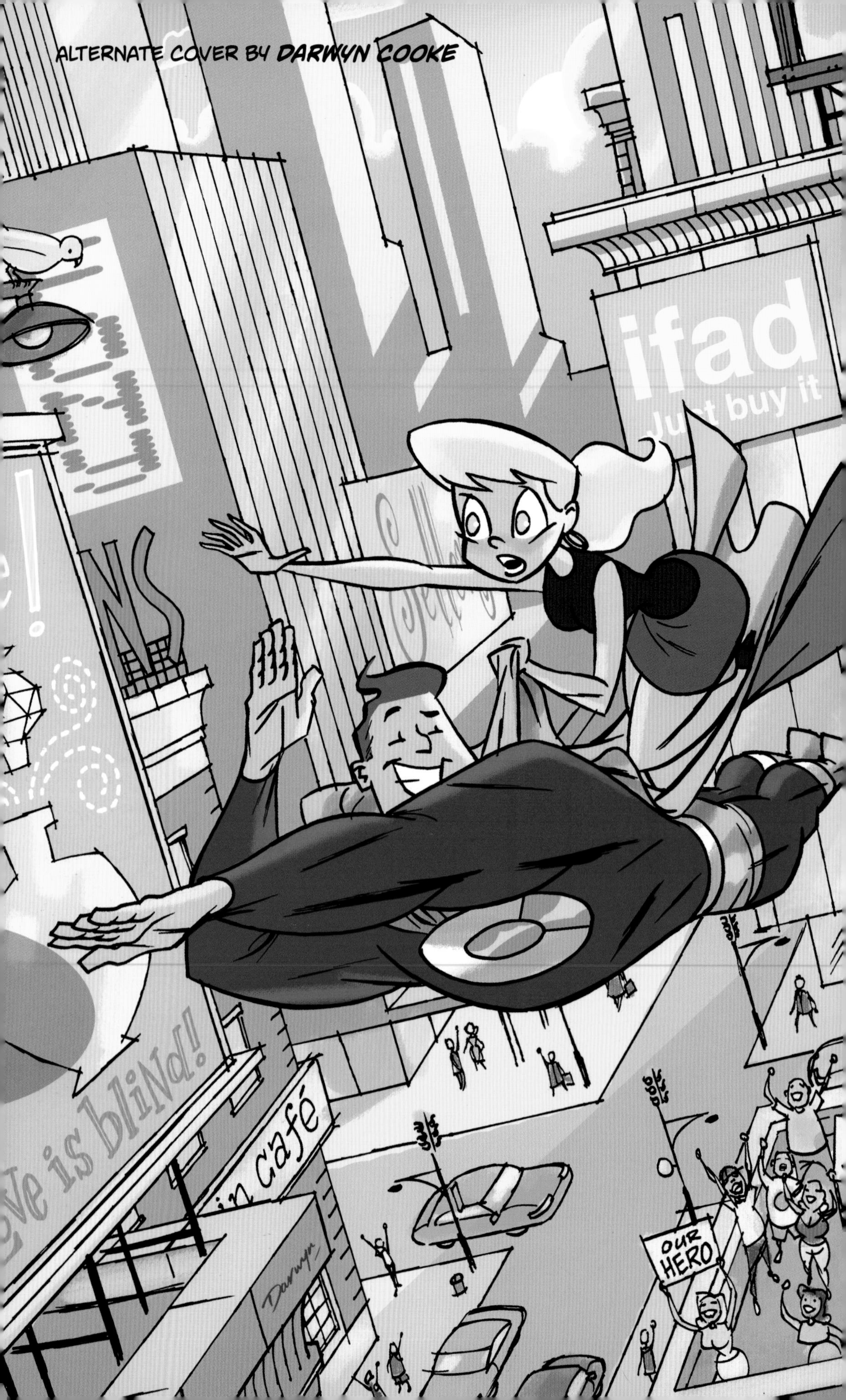
ifad
Just buy it
in café
OUR HERO
Darwyn
ALTERNATE COVER BY *DARWYN COOKE*

CHRONOPOLIS...

How's the *house* coming, Mark?

Slowly.

The bedroom and living room are almost done. Everything else may have to wait until *after* we move in.

A house is *never* done. It's *always* a work in progress.

So I'm learning.

Abby's *Dad* has been great about helping, though.

Glad to hear he's getting used to having a *super son-in-law.*

It's costing me weekly trips to Ireland for *fresh Guinness,* but that man can *spackle.*

I'm just surprised how much being a home-owner is *changing* my heroing outlook.

Really? How so?

Well, having actually *patched* a wall, I may think twice the next time I think I should crash *though* one.

Hang on, that guy looks *shifty.*

You're just saying that because he's wearing a *Yankees cap.*

Well-- yeah.

I *guess* he's okay.

So, how's *Abby* handling everything?

Not bad. She's a mix of *excited and stressed.*

I'm sure *you* know how those *Type A* people can be, Paul.

Very funny.

We *have* had a couple conflicts about setting up the new place, though.

She thought she was getting the *whole* walk-in closet, didn't she?

Hey, my uniforms have to go *some-where!*

87

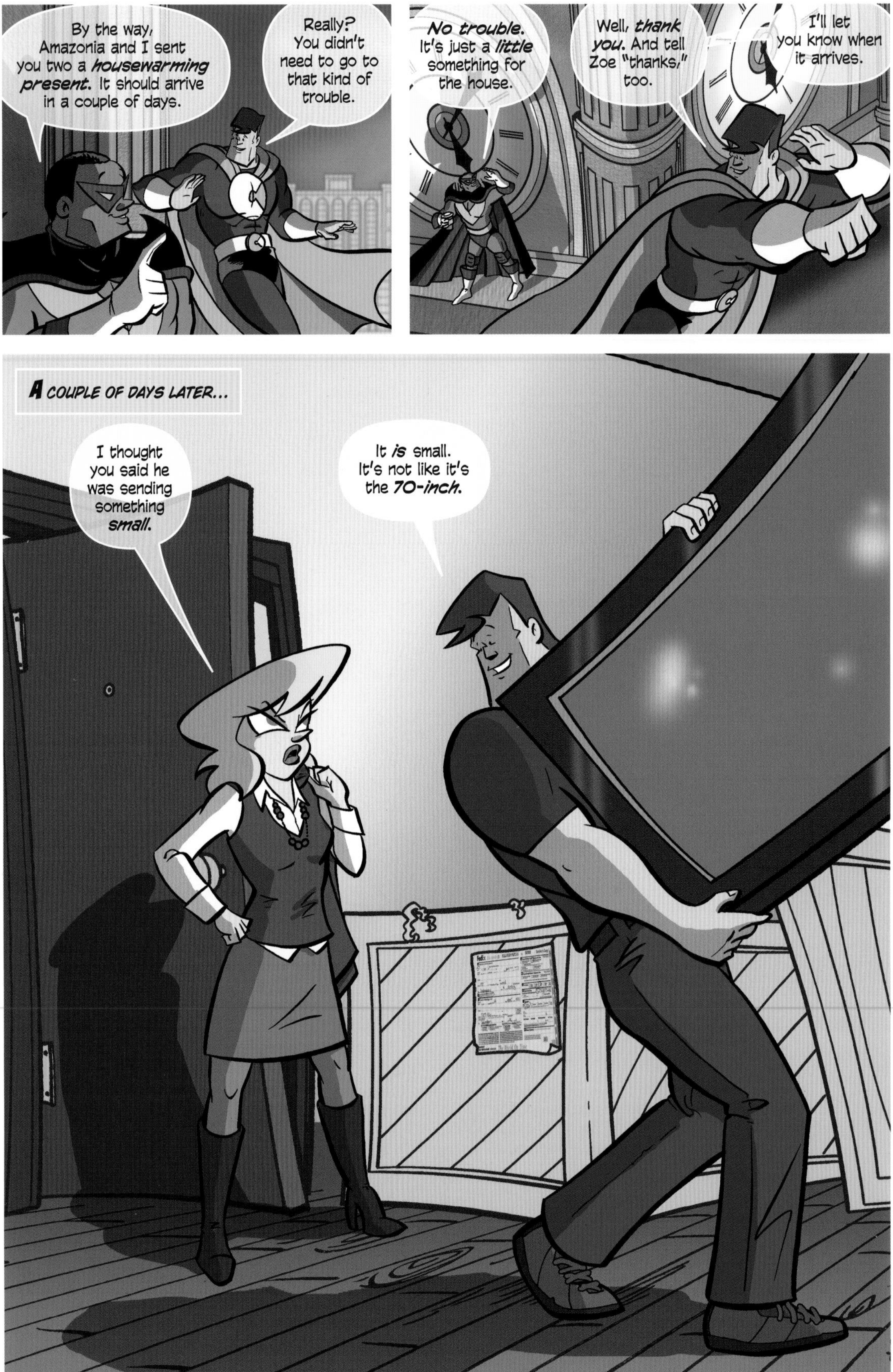

By the way, Amazonia and I sent you two a *housewarming present.* It should arrive in a couple of days.
Really? You didn't need to go to that kind of trouble.
No trouble. It's just a *little* something for the house.
Well, *thank you.* And tell Zoe "thanks," too.
I'll let you know when it arrives.
A COUPLE OF DAYS LATER...
I thought you said he was sending something *small.*
It *is* small. It's not like it's the *70-inch.*

What *else* is in here?

It's an *M&K sound system.* Same thing Lucasfilm uses at Skywalker Ranch.

Lovely.

Paul says they're good enough that my super hearing won't pick up that *subsonic hum* I hear from other speakers.

Hello. What's this?

I guess he got sick of hearing me *complain* about it.

The Adventures of Tom Sawyer... *first edition?*

ABBY—
DIDN'T FORGET YOU!
—Paul

I have to say, that deductive mind of his can pick out some *great presents.*

I *can't* argue with that.

Looks like we got some mail that *isn't* high tech, too.

Oh, yeah. I got so distracted by the TV, I didn't even look over it.

Anything *good* in there?

Just a "Last Reminder" invite to my *St. John's Academy class reunion.*

You know, now that you mention it, um...

...you don't still have your old *school uniform,* do you?

God! What *is* it with you men and *outfits?*

Really? I wear a *cape* and you're surprised I have a thing for *costumes?*

So, are we *going* to your reunion?

I'm *not* sure. I need to think about it.

Hey, you finished painting the *bedroom!*

Mark, it looks *wonderful!*

You *think* so? I'm not sure.

All I see are the *little mistakes*, I guess.

I'm sure the eyes of the craftsman are *always* the most critical--

--especially when those eyes have *microscopic vision.*

THEN...

--so I was thinking about it and, *aside* from fixing the *hideous color*--

--I thought that if we *knock out* that wall, it'd really open the room up.

Yeah. You're *absolutely* right.

So we--

B O O M!

Mark! What did you do?

Knocked out the wall. I thought we were *agreed.*

Yes, but-- what if that had been a *load-bearing wall?*

Oh, *please.* With my line of work, I *know* what a load-bearing wall looks like.

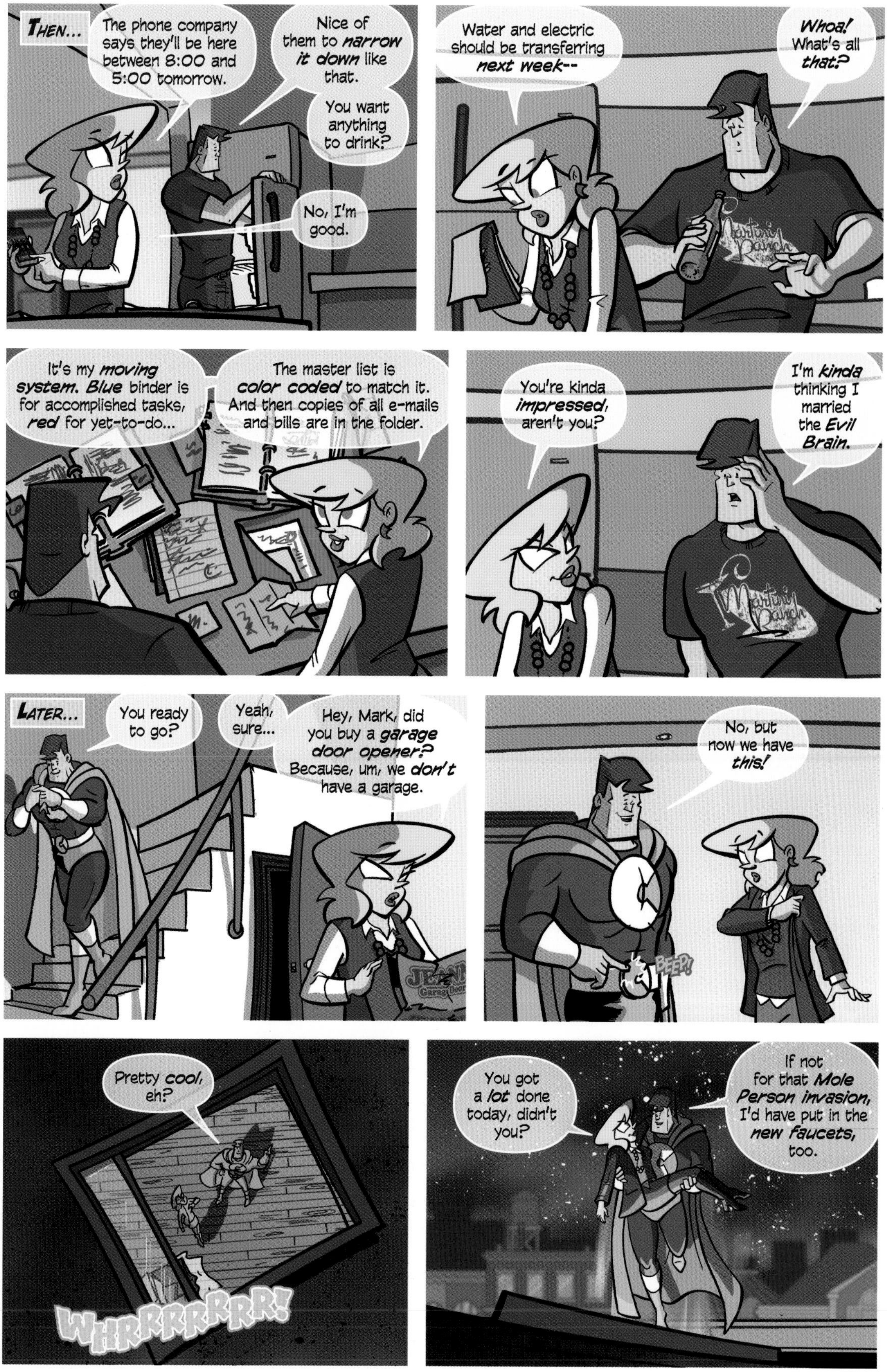
THEN...
The phone company says they'll be here between 8:00 and 5:00 tomorrow.
Nice of them to narrow it down like that.
You want anything to drink?
No, I'm good.
Water and electric should be transferring next week--
Whoa! What's all that?
Martini Ranch
It's my moving system. Blue binder is for accomplished tasks, red for yet-to-do...
The master list is color coded to match it. And then copies of all e-mails and bills are in the folder.
You're kinda impressed, aren't you?
I'm kinda thinking I married the Evil Brain.
Martini Ranch
LATER...
You ready to go?
Yeah, sure...
Hey, Mark, did you buy a garage door opener? Because, um, we don't have a garage.
No, but now we have this!
BEEP!
Pretty cool, eh?
WHRRRRRRR!
You got a lot done today, didn't you?
If not for that Mole Person invasion, I'd have put in the new faucets, too.

THE NEXT DAY...

So, *why* are you on the fence about going to your high school reunion, Abby?

Oh, *lots* of reasons, Jason.

My time in high school wasn't *exacly* a *hit parade* of my best moments, you know. *Lots* of teen angst.

I'm just not sure I want to *wallow* in that pool of memories for a night.

I get that. I remember how tough *my* high school years were.

It's a struggle for identity and acceptance in most cases. Coming to terms with being *gay* on top of that just made it *all the harder.*

I'm sorry though, I cut you off. What was *your* heart-rending angst about?

You *do* have a way of putting things in *perspective*, you know that?

But don't let *me* talk you out of going to your reunion, Abby. It's not like I've even *had* one yet.

That's *right.* Sometimes I forget how much *younger* you are.

Yes, but I am *wise* beyond my *few years.*

You know, it *would* be kind of nice to show Mark where I went to high school.

Plus, there are a couple of people that I'd *love* to find out what they're up to now.

Isn't that what *Facebook* is for?

Not *everyone's* on Facebook, Jason.

Who's not-- oh, yeah. *Old* people. Sorry about that.

One more crack like that and my *next* status update will say "*Looking for new employee.*"

LATER, IN PARIS...

Sorry I'm late, Charlotte.

Don't worry about it, Paul.

You *are* buying now, of course.

Well, of course.

But, before anything else, I need to *apologize*. I know I haven't been around as much as I should be.

I was trying to remember, and I've don't think I've been to visit since *before* your sister's wedding.

I've just been *so busy*--

You mean *getting busy*.

With *Amazonia*.

Hey, that's--

Accurate?

I was going to say "*beside the point*."

So, what prompted you to ask me to lunch?

Well, you're right, it *has* been a while.

But I also need to ask a *favor*.

My senior thesis is on German artists of the 1960s. Right now I'm focusing on an artist named *Diethelm Auerbach*.

He only did about thirty paintings. *Most* are in museums, but there are a couple that are in *private collections*.

If I could actually *see* one of those, it'd help me out a *lot*.

And you need me to find out if one of my *rich friends* has an Auerbach?

No, you *doofus*--

Oh, God, *I* own one, don't I?

You've got it right above your *fireplace!*

93

AND THEN...

Paul, how is it with *your* memory you didn't realize you had that painting?

I let *Mrs. O'Lonergan* handle most of the household purchases.

I know *who* Auerbach is. I just never realized she *bought* one of his paintings.

Oh, Mrs. O'Lonergan. I've *missed* her.

She's missed *you*, too. She was *thrilled* when I let her know you were coming to visit.

Wait, she *knows* I'm coming? Does that mean--

Yes. It *does*.

Snickerdoodles! *Squeee!*

LATER...

Are things going well with *Amazonia?*

Amazingly so.

It's always a little *daunting* to get involved with one of your friends--especially someone who dated your best friend--but we're becoming a pretty good couple.

I can't tell you how wonderful it is to be with someone that knows the *complete me*. There's no *hiding*, no *lying*. Just us.

I'm really *glad* we got together at your sister's wedding.

You mean the wedding where you chose *her* wedding-and-liquor-fueled hookup request over mine?

Um, *yeah.*

Is this going to be a *thing?*

Only when I *need something.*

Emotional intimidation. *Lovely.*

I learned from the best, Oh Scary One.

THE LACROIX MANSION...

--and the whole thing was a *hologram*.

Amazing!

Welcome back, Mr. LaCroix.

Thank you, Mrs. O'Lonergan.

Would you be so kind as to *take care* of Charlotte while I change into something less "*creature of the night*"?

Of course.

It's so *lovely* to have you back, Charlotte.

Thanks, Mrs. O.

You know, just by happenstance, there's a fresh batch of *cookies* cooling in the kitchen.

Oh, really?

Hey, *I'd* like a cookie, *too!*

And *I'd* like you to stick to your prescribed *meal plan* while you're out of the mansion--

--but from the French latte on your breath, I can tell we're *both* going to be *disappointed*.

LATER...

So *this* is the painting I've heard so much about.

Yup.

It's one of his *early* pieces. His brush strokes are a lot more *tentative* than in his later work.

Yes, but his *distinctive* color pallette has already emerged.

You can see how much *Monet* influenced him, too.

You think? I was going to say *Bazille*.

You really know a *lot* about art, don't you?

You fight *Master Stroke* enough times and you pick some things up.

--yes, Brother Cillian, I think he'd be a *perfect addition* to the *Order*.

Excuse me a moment. I have an *unexpected guest*.

Good evening, Mrs. O'Lonergan. Is *Paul* around?

Yes, Miss Amazonia. He's in the *east wing great room*, entertaining Ms. Tennyson.

Abby's here?

No, her sister *Charlotte*.

Oh.

Brother Cillian, I'm going to need to *call you back*.

I have a feeling my evening is about to devolve into a *British farce*.

Hello, you two.

Hello, Amazonia.

Zoe! I thought you were doing that interview with *Ellen* today.

I *was*, but they needed to bump me to *tomorrow*.

Such is show biz.

So, what's going on *here?*

Charlotte needed to see one of my paintings to write her *senior art history thesis*.

So I brought her by to see it *in person*.

Can I get you a glass?

Sure.

You know, none of *my* study sessions at the Academy involved *wine*.

Benefits of a *Parisian education*.

96

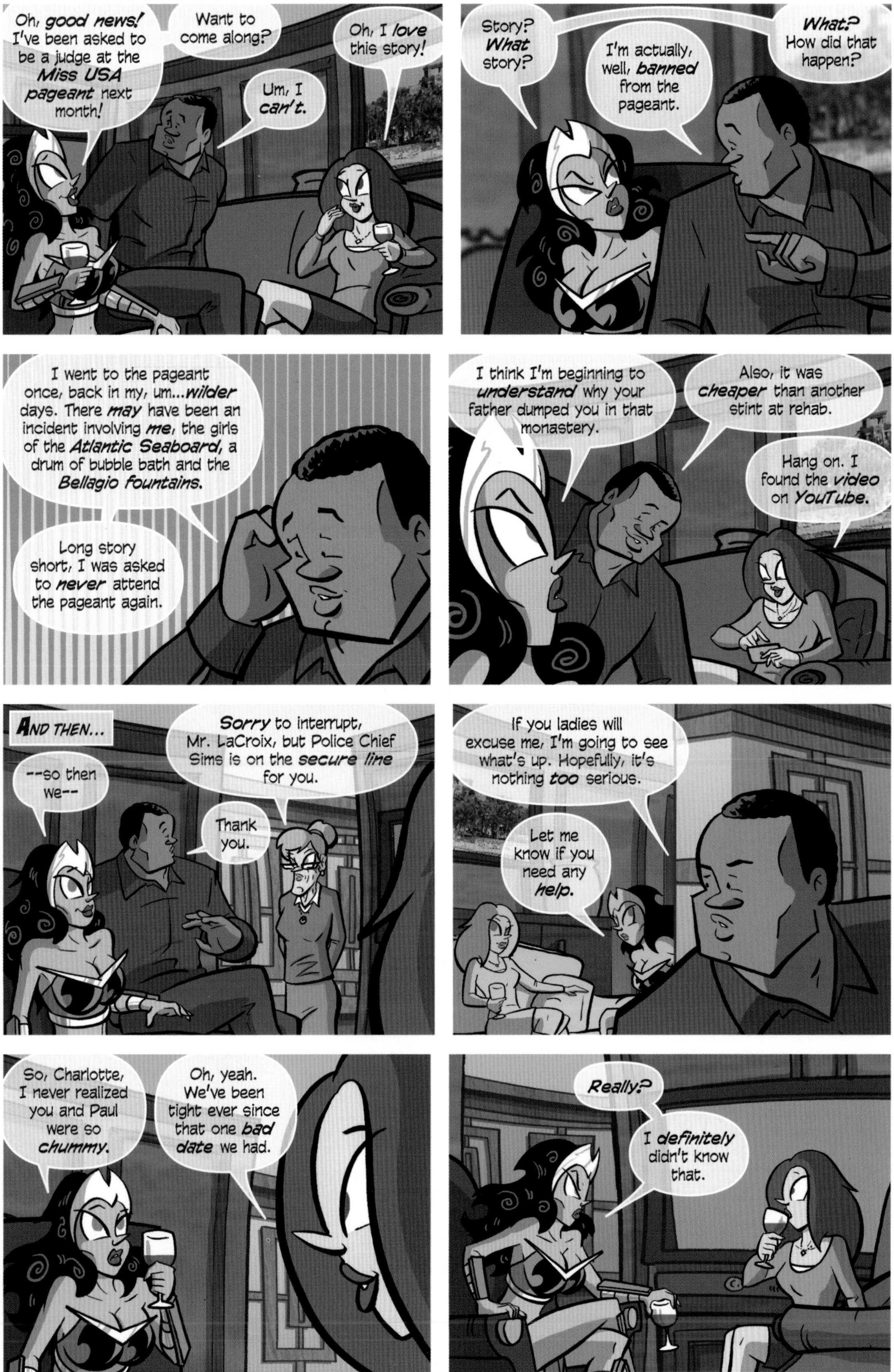
Oh, good news! I've been asked to be a judge at the Miss USA pageant next month!
Want to come along?
Um, I can't.
Oh, I love this story!
Story? What story?
I'm actually, well, banned from the pageant.
What? How did that happen?
I went to the pageant once, back in my, um...wilder days. There may have been an incident involving me, the girls of the Atlantic Seaboard, a drum of bubble bath and the Bellagio fountains.
Long story short, I was asked to never attend the pageant again.
I think I'm beginning to understand why your father dumped you in that monastery.
Also, it was cheaper than another stint at rehab.
Hang on. I found the video on YouTube.
AND THEN...
--so then we--
Sorry to interrupt, Mr. LaCroix, but Police Chief Sims is on the secure line for you.
Thank you.
If you ladies will excuse me, I'm going to see what's up. Hopefully, it's nothing too serious.
Let me know if you need any help.
So, Charlotte, I never realized you and Paul were so chummy.
Oh, yeah. We've been tight ever since that one bad date we had.
Really?
I definitely didn't know that.

You and Paul *went out?*

Just *once.* And it was a horrible flaming train wreck of an evening.

But then we stopped trying to *date* and just started *talking.*

It turned out we got along great... as *friends.*

Plus, we *really* liked ragging on Mark and Abby.

Well, I can understand that.

Paul's become one of my *best friends.* It's because of his encouragement that I'm finishing my degree.

Well, that and him arranging that *scholar-ship.*

Wait, so he's *paying* for your college, too?

Okay, you *may* be focusing on the wrong part there.

Amazonia, you *know* you have nothing to worry about from me.

Heck, at the wedding I gave Paul the *same* drunken proposition you did and--

WHAT?

--and he didn't tell you that either, did he?

No, he *didn't.* But don't worry, we're going to talk about it *now.*

Amazonia, wait! You're *missing the point*--

Another cookie, dear?

Mrs. O, you always know just when to--

--wait, you were watching on the *security feed,* weren't you?

Better than *EastEnders,* dear.

98

PAUL!

Zoe, I was *just* going to have Mrs. O'Longeran send for you--

Well, I'm here *now*.

What's wrong?

How could you *not* tell me about you and Charlotte at the wedding? Or that you *dated* her?

Anything *else* you're hiding about her?

Zoe, Charlotte and I are *just friends*. But you're right that I didn't tell you about her "offer" at the wedding. That was *nothing more* than the combination of the wedding and alcohol.

Besides, I figured you'd just get *upset*.

Well, I *am* upset.

So I was *right*.

Are you *trying* to get hit? Because I can *do* that.

Zoe, I *never* realized that you didn't know Charlotte and I were friends.

But I should have found *some time* to tell you about the night of the wedding, and I'm *sorry* about that.

And, I'm *not* trying to get out of this, but Chief Sims had called to let me know that the *Evil Brain* is here in Chronopolis.

We can talk more en route, but we *need* to *find him* and stop whatever malfeasance he has planned.

Unless you'd rather me handle this solo. I can take the Airblade--

Don't be foolish, it's the *Evil Brain*. I'll fly you, and we can talk *on the way*.

Now, *let's talk*.

This *may* have been a mistake.

Zoe, I didn't *mean* to hide my friendship with Charlotte from you.

I *haven't* spent a lot of time with her since you and I got together, mostly because I've been spending my time with *you*.

And *yes*, I had a choice between you and her at the wedding.

I chose *you*, and it was very much the *right choice*.

But, I've also *neglected* Charlotte since then, and that's been a mistake. That's not the kind of *friend*--the kind of *person*--I want to be.

So, I'll do *whatever* I can to make you comfortable with Charlotte and my friendship.

But she's going to *stay* my friend.

And if I have a *problem* with that?

Then *we're* going to have a problem.

Paul, I came over tonight and saw you drinking wine with a cute girl that you have a history with.

You can see why I'd take that *badly*, right? I mean, it's not like you don't have a *reputation*.

Had a reputation. *Past tense*.

People *change*, Zoe. I'm not the *hard-partying womanizer* that I used to be.

The same way *you're* not the petulant attention-seeking princess you were when I *first* met you.

Which is good, because I wouldn't be in *love* with that woman.

So, if you're willing to *trust* me, we can work through this. Otherwise--

--let me *go*.

I'm *not* about to let you go.

No, seriously, let me *drop*.

It's just a *hunch*, I'm guessing the Evil Brain might be in that building with the *missile* mounted on the roof.

MEANWHILE...

I'm still *not sure* about this.

Come on, it'll be *fun*. See some old friends, hear some old songs, have a *life-affirming epiphany*--

This isn't a *Nineties high-school reunion movie*, honey.

I think you're looking forward to this *more* than *me*.

High school was just all *sunshine* and *rainbows* for you, wasn't it?

Oh, yeah, puberty *and* developing super powers. It was a breeze.

Well, I'm sure the *magnetic resonance vision* that came with the latter helped with the former.

I have no idea what you're talking about.

Of course not.

Beth Parker! I haven't seen you in years!

Abby Tennyson! How are you?

It's Abby *Spencer*, now. This is my husband *Mark*.

Are you still the manager at *Foodlane?*

No, I moved over to that Krauser's on Fillmore. You know, the one we used to steal *milk crates* from?

Hey, I get done here in twenty minutes. Want to grab a *smoke* and catch up?

No, *sorry*. I quit back in college. But I'll see you inside.

Tonight's just going to be *one big learning experience*, isn't it?

It's probably best if you think of it as my *secret identity*.

Anything you want to *warn me* about?

Look, Mark, I was *really* different in high school.

I got *great* grades and my teachers *liked* me. So, I got away with indulging my *impulsive side.*

Hey, *Skins,* great to see, you!

You, too, *Curves.*

Should I ask?

It's probably best that you *don't.*

LATER...

--wait, so Sister Mary Alice is still *alive?* She was *ancient* when she taught *us!*

I know, but I did Career Day here last month, and there she was. She hasn't changed *a bit.*

I ran into your *brother,* too. His presentation was *really* popular.

Oh, yeah, I think he mentioned that.

You know, my husband and I watch his *sports report* all the time.

We love it when he puts on the *penguin costume* and does those *"Cool Picks."*

Yes, we're all *very* proud.

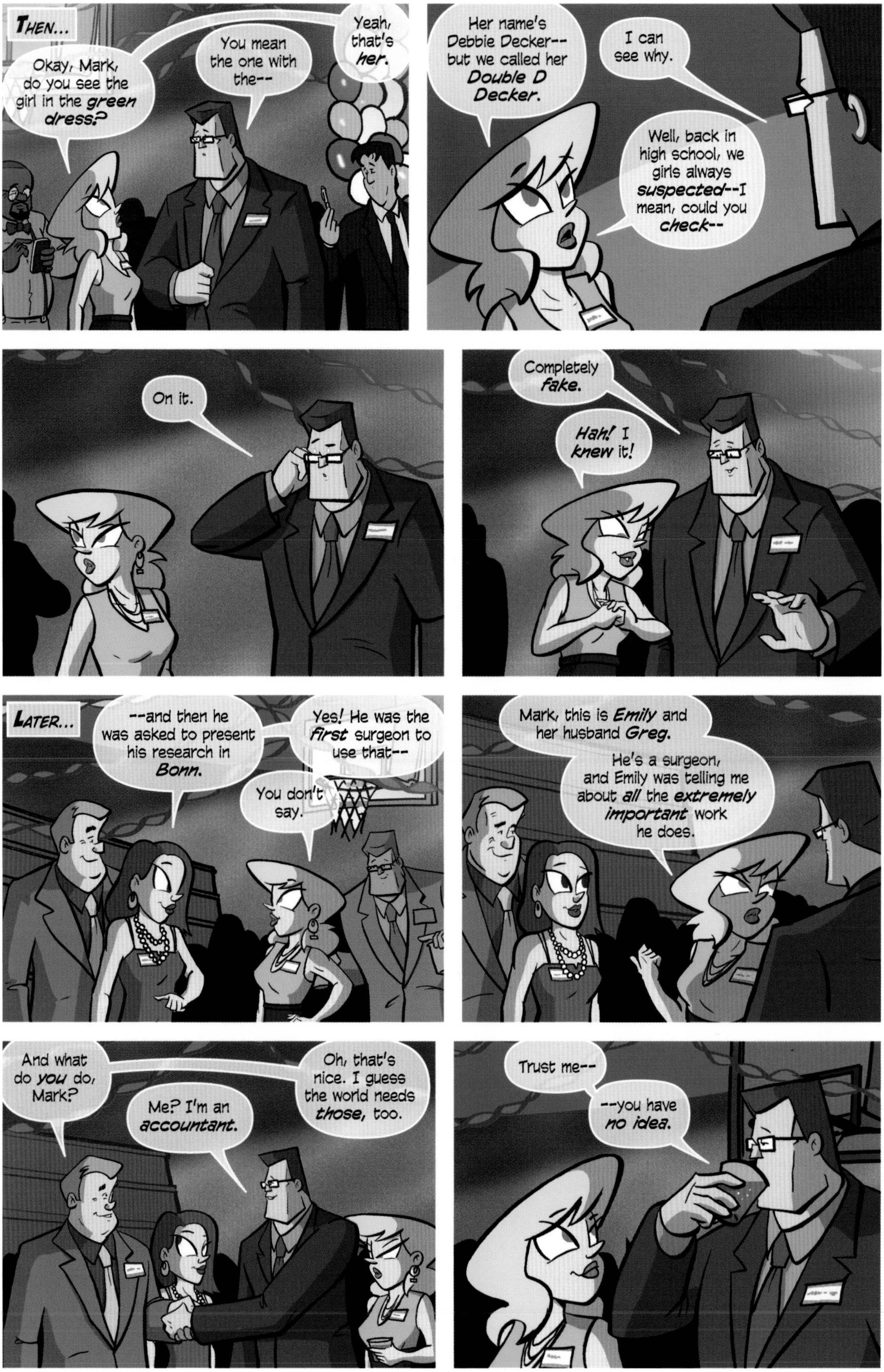
THEN...
Okay, Mark, do you see the girl in the green dress?
You mean the one with the--
Yeah, that's her.
Her name's Debbie Decker--but we called her Double D Decker.
I can see why.
Well, back in high school, we girls always suspected--I mean, could you check--
On it.
Completely fake.
Hah! I knew it!
LATER...
--and then he was asked to present his research in Bonn.
Yes! He was the first surgeon to use that--
You don't say.
Mark, this is Emily and her husband Greg.
He's a surgeon, and Emily was telling me about all the extremely important work he does.
And what do you do, Mark?
Me? I'm an accountant.
Oh, that's nice. I guess the world needs those, too.
Trust me--
--you have no idea.

LATER...

Whoops! That's my *phone.*

Would you excuse me?

BLEEP! BLEEP!

BLEEP! BLEEP!

Darkblade? What is it?

We've got a problem. The *Evil Brain*--and *yes*, he got away--came to town to buy a multiple warhead *missile* from Weaponella.

We busted them up, but he managed to get the *launch* off.

Where's it headed?

That's the thing. He built a *genetic targeting system*-- and he stole a sample of *your* DNA.

You've got about *three minutes* before it *finds* you.

Abby--

It's fine, *go.*

How'd you know?

Um, because I've *met* you?

I don't know-- that missile packs quite a *punch.* Should we call someone *else*, too?

Crusader says he's got it. So he's got it.

I trust *my* friends.

≷Sigh!≷ Fine, you've *made your point.*

Can we agree that *you* handled this poorly, and *I* reacted just as bad?

Deal.

Speaking of which, we should probably get back. We *did* leave her in the lurch.

Sims's men can clean up here.

Maybe you could invite *me* out with the two of you next time. It'd probably help.

And then you could see for yourself that *nothing's going on*, too?

Well, think of it as trust-- but *verify.*

104

MEANWHILE...

Is anyone sitting here?

No, it's--

Oh my God! *Ted!*

Hi, Abby. How have you been?

I've, uh, been fine. How have *you* been?

I haven't talked to you since— *since...*

Since you *dumped me* for Steve Hatcher the *week before Prom?*

Uh, yeah.

Ted, I'm *so sorry.* I thought about calling or writing to apologize, but I didn't know what to say.

Honestly, the thought of running into you *almost* kept me from coming tonight.

Well, I'm *glad* you came.

We never *talked* after we broke up. And then we went off to college and never *saw* each other.

I had always *thought* that it would have been nice if we'd talked afterwards. Maybe a little closure would have made it *less painful.*

But you *did* get over it, right? I didn't emotionally *scar* you or anything, did I?

Are you kidding? I was a *wreck.* Freshman year I made dark and moody an *art form.*

Fortunately, Alyson was *into* dark and moody at the time.

Hi.

105

So, I can stop feeling *guilty*?

Really, don't give it another thought. Everything worked out *just fine*.

It's not just finding the *right person*, it's finding them at the *right time*.

But what about you? I thought I saw you *with* someone--

That's my husband *Mark*. We just got married this summer.

Unfortunately, there was some *work crisis*, and he stepped out to handle it.

You know, Ted's office does that to him *all the time*. I *hate* it. What, is the world going to *end* without them?

Well, you *never know*.

MEANWHILE...

I just have to *refuel* the Airblade and run the *pre-flight check*, and then I can get you back to Paris, Charlotte.

Thanks, Paul.

I think I owe you an *apology*, Charlotte. I shouldn't have gotten *jealous* of you and Paul.

Don't *worry* about it, Amazonia.

You had *every reason* to be jealous.

Excuse me?

Um, clearly I need to explain that.

Look, I don't know if you and Paul have exchanged the *L-word* yet, but it's definitely something *substantial*, right?

Yes, that's true.

Well, any person that makes you think...substantially, is going to be a person that you think is pretty *amazing*. Smart, funny, whatever it is *you're* looking for.

So you have this special guy and you start to wonder *how* no one snapped him up before? After all, *you* see how great he is. It's *obvious*.

But then you start to worry that maybe someone else *will* see how great he is.

And *that's* when you get jealous. I mean, how can you *not?*

You sound like you're talking from *experience*.

Sadly, though, mostly the experience of being the *other woman*.

The Airblade is *refueled* and ready whenever *you* are, Charlotte.

You know, you *could* come with us--

No, you really *should* have some time with your *friend*.

Mrs. O, it's been *so nice* seeing you again.

You, too, child. *Please* make sure to visit again.

Oh, and I slipped a bag of *cookies* behind your seat, too.

You're the *best!*

Take care, dear.

See you soon.

Thanks for *everything*. See you later.

Paul, are those two going to be okay by *them-selves?*

Oh, they should be *fine*.

And, if not, the place locks down at anything over a *2.0 tremor*.

ELSEWHERE...

Please tell me you didn't come out here to smoke.

No, don't worry. Those days are long gone.

So then, what brings you out to the bleachers?

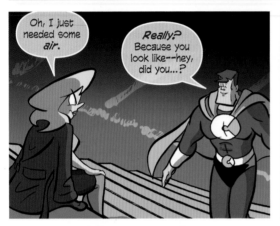

Oh, I just needed some air.

Really? Because you look like--hey, did you...?

Yes. ⟫Grumble!⟪ I had a life-affirming epiphany.

Hah! I knew it!

You've got Nineties tunes running through your head right now, don't you?

"Every Morning" by Sugar Ray.

So what happened?

Every once in a while I think how great it would have been if we'd met sooner.

It would have spared us each some heartbreaks and lonely nights. And Amazonia.

But I was talking to someone I used to date and I realized just how intricate life can be.

You know, if we'd met in high school, I probably wouldn't have given you the time of day.

I'm glad I found you when I could appreciate you.

Well, I'd like to get *back* in there and see a couple more people before we leave.

You should *probably* change for that.

Yeah, *probably.*

Give me *just a minute.*

So, did everything go *okay* tonight for you?

The city's not a *smouldering crater*, so I'm going to say "yes."

Just an *average* Saturday night, then.

What *was* the emergency tonight?

Oh, the Evil Brain let loose a *nuclear missile* pretty much headed right for us.

See, that's *not fair!* I have the *coolest* husband out of anyone here, and I *don't* get to *brag about you.*

Everyone here owes you *their* life.

Yeah, I *suppose.* But really, the Evil Brain was just trying to kill *the Crusader.*

So no one would have been in danger *at all* if not for me.

Oh, well, in that case *Shana Johnston* has the coolest husband. He was on *The Real World* season twelve.

The *Vegas* year? Yeah, I can't compete with *that.*

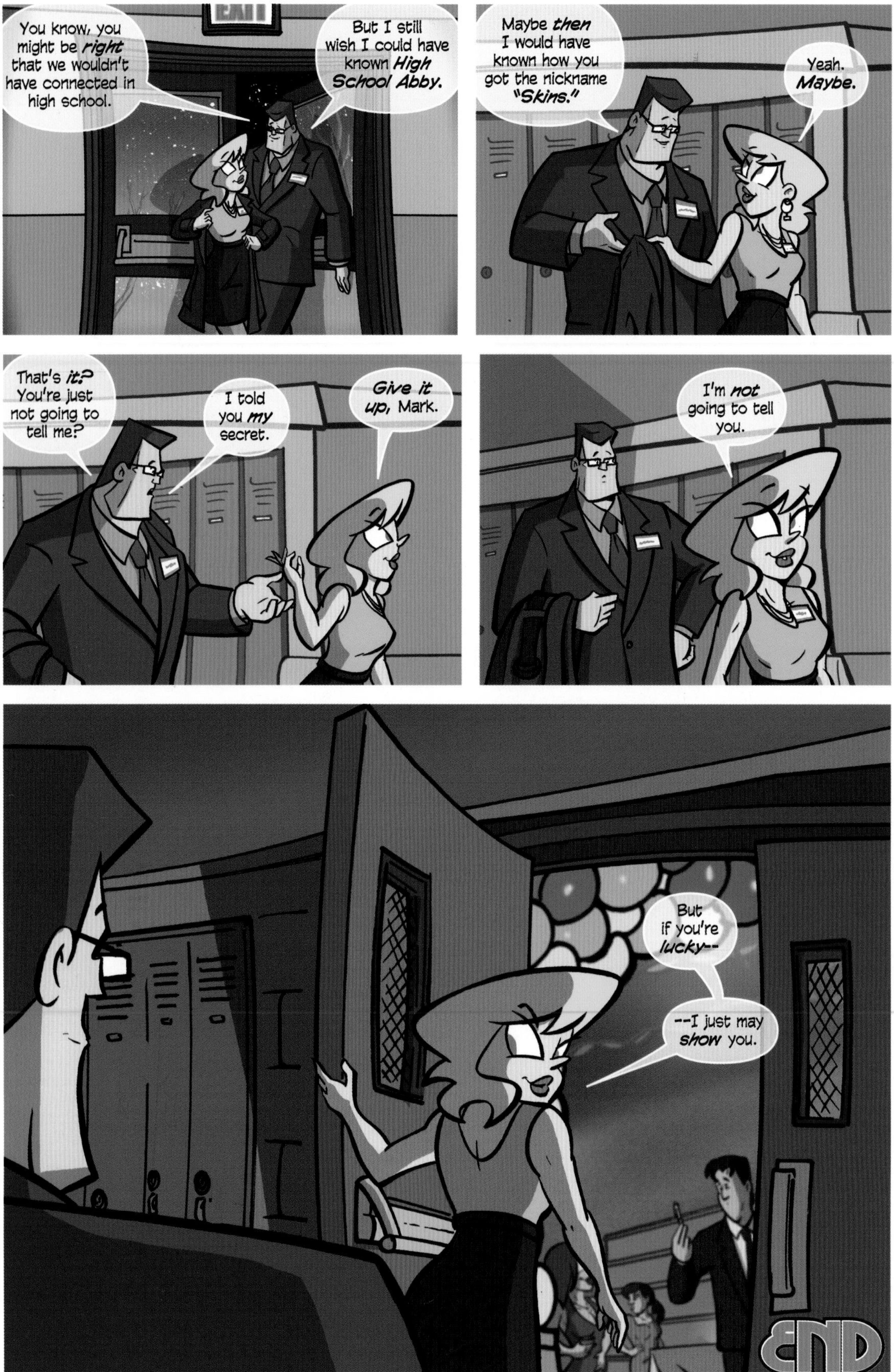
You know, you might be *right* that we wouldn't have connected in high school.
But I still wish I could have known *High School Abby.*
Maybe *then* I would have known how you got the nickname *"Skins."*
Yeah. *Maybe.*
That's *it?* You're just not going to tell me?
I told you *my* secret.
Give it up, Mark.
I'm *not* going to tell you.
But if you're *lucky*--
--I just may *show* you.
END

CHAPTER 5
YOU KNOW THIS IS CHEATING, RIGHT?
QUIET! YOU'RE IN A TRANCE!
DECO CIT
TALENT SHO

LOVE AND CAPES
Ever After

"LOVE" COVER

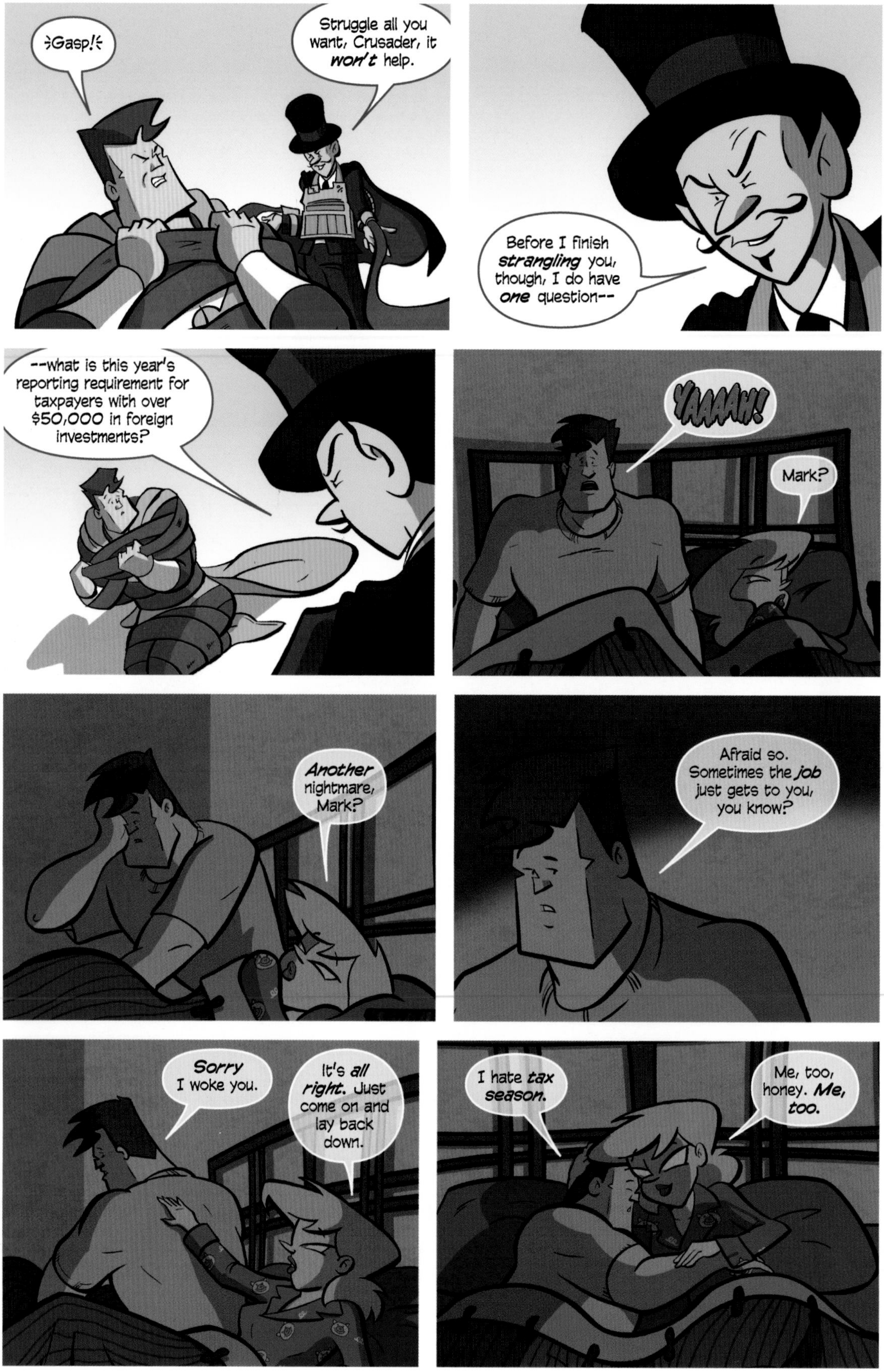

Gasp!
Struggle all you want, Crusader, it *won't* help.
Before I finish *strangling* you, though, I do have *one* question--
--what is this year's reporting requirement for taxpayers with over $50,000 in foreign investments?
YAAAAH!
Mark?
Another nightmare, Mark?
Afraid so. Sometimes the *job* just gets to you, you know?
Sorry I woke you.
It's *all right.* Just come on and lay back down.
I hate *tax season.*
Me, too, honey. *Me, too.*

LATER...

--so with Congress taking *so long* to agree on the *tax compromise*, it delayed a lot of the information Mark *needed* to get started.

I can see where that would mess things up.

Yeah, between that and his *other* job, he's *really* burning the candle at both ends.

Wait, *what* other job?

D'oh!

Um, well--

--you know, being married to *me*. It can be a *full-time* job.

Oh, yeah. I can *totally* see that.

STILL LATER...

Please come again, sir.

Jason, I'm taking off for a bit. I have to go to the *Merchant Association luncheon*.

Really? I thought you told me that group was a... *how* did you put it... "a glorified *selling circle* run by incompetent *windbags*."

Oh, it *still is*.

But now that I *own the building* and am landlord for three *other businesses* in the Square, I kind of feel like I *need* to be there.

Plus, maybe it'll help me find a tenant for my *empty* storefront.

So, what time do you want your *fake emergency call* to get you out of there?

I'll text you once I find out if they're serving anything good for *dessert*.

115

THE LUNCHEON...

--and I pass out *coupons* at the store.

That's great, Jim.

Abby, care to share some of *your* marketing secrets?

Oh, I probably don't do anything much differently than everyone else.

I bring *authors* into the store whenever I can, and I run *specials*...

Thank y--

I just started up a *Twitter* account so I could do daily *book recommendations*.

I've got the account linked to my *Facebook page*, too. We're also *sponsoring* the Morning Show book chat segment and--

They made me president.

THEN...

So, what's going to be your *first official act*, Madame President?

I was thinking about organizing a *sidewalk sale/street fair*. It'd be a nice event to draw people down here.

Oh, that's a *great* idea!

I'm *so glad* to hear you say that.

You know, I think I liked it better when you didn't know how to *delegate*.

That's what you get for being more *competent* than my *sister*.

CHRONOPOLIS...

So, do I need to rotate you off Monitor Duty until the end of tax season?

Oh, no. In fact, I could pull a couple of *extra* shifts. Being stuck at a desk is good for getting work done.

That is, as long as those of you planetside don't mind *picking up the slack.*

That's a fair trade. After all, you *do* handle the League's books and taxes.

The *books*, yeah. But we *don't pay taxes.*

Not *at all?*

Nope. No controlling tax authority.

Why do you think I insisted we base ourselves on a *satellite?*

THEN...

I just found out my *parents* are coming into town next week.

Really? What's the occasion?

A *sad one.* One of Dad's friends from business school passed away.

I'm *sorry* to hear that.

If he'd died just a couple of months *earlier*, he would have skated on the *Estate Tax.*

Seriously, dude? That's *dark*. And that's coming from a *creature of the night.*

Gah! See how this job makes you think sometimes?

This is why we need *tax reform!*

Say, will this be the *first time* your parents meet *Amazonia?*

You know, *yes*, it will.

Have you *thought* about that? I mean, Zoe's great, but I know from *experience* that meeting parents is *not* her strong suit.

She can be kind of...well, you know...*Zoe.*

Yeah, I know what you mean. And I have a *plan.*

I should *never* have doubted.

Care to share it?

DECO CITY...

Okay, *you* may be immune to the cold, but *I'm* not.

Let's go *inside.*

When was the last time you were over, Zoe?

I don't know. It's been a *couple of months* at least.

Then you *haven't* seen--

--that we've *finally finished moving in.*

So, you're looking for *advice* on meeting Paul's parents?

What do you know about them?

Well, Paul's always had a *contentious* relationship with his father--due in no small part to the senior LaCroix arranging to have Paul *kidnapped* by *Irish warrior priests.*

Paul knows he needed the forced redemption, but it's still a *sore point.*

Plus, I'm not sure Paul ever forgave him for *remarrying* after his mother passed away.

It's *hard* replacing a little boy's mother.

Wow. They'd make for a great episode of *"Jerry Springer,"* wouldn't they?

It'd certainly have the *best* fights.

Well, in my experience, it's *not* so much about getting the parents to *like* you as not giving them a reason to *dislike* you.

So, it's playing *defense?*

Exactly. You don't want to come on too strong.

And, in *your* case, you might want to dress a little more... *conservatively.*

Really? In my culture, when we meet our prospective mate's parents, we wear our most *revealing* clothing.

We want to showcase our *health* and *virility*--

--and, you look a little *shocked.*

Only that you could wear *less* and still call it *"clothing."*

LATER...

--then we--

--um--

Abby, is it *snowing* in here?

Hello, ladies.

How are you both this evening?

Mark, I thought we had an *agreement* about the skylight.

Right. Don't use it when it's *raining.*

Snow is frozen rain!

Oh, yeah.

Sorry.

THEN...

You know, I think I'm going to take off, too, Abby.

All right.

But don't worry. I'll use the *stairs.*

Thanks. I appreciate that.

And I appreciate all your advice.

I probably *will* take you up on your offer to help me pick out an outfit, too.

We could go shopping in *Paris.* Maybe pick up *Charlotte,* make a day of it?

Sure, sounds good.

Yep, this is *exactly* how I pictured married life when I was a little girl.

120

THE NEXT MORNING...

Mark?

Honey, did you come to bed *at all* last night?

Hmm? Oh, *no*. I'm still churning on these taxes.

It's okay, though, I don't actually *need* sleep.

Right, but I thought you needed occasional *dream time* to keep from going *insane*.

Don't worry, I've got that covered.

Darkblade will take me down if I go *crazy*.

Well, as long as you have a *plan*.

LATER...

Mark! I made breakfast!

I know you have a *lot* to do, but you need to *take a break* every now and then.

ZOOM

Thanks, dear.

⊰Sigh!⊱ I'm sure those were a very *refreshing* two seconds.

THEN...

TAPTAPTAPTAPTAP... ...TAPTAPTAP

TAPTAPTAPTAPTAPTAPTAP

TAPTAPTAP CRASH!

LATER...

Mark, I just-- Whoa! What's this?

Sometimes spreading everything out like this helps me see the whole financial picture.

Clients like these are the bane of my existence. They think "organized" means everything in the same shoebox.

Hey, that's how I brought you my taxes. Did you say that about me?

No, but you also rocked a skirt better than Mr. MacCosh.

He's Scottish, dear. That was a kilt.

And yet I think my point stands.

THE NEXT DAY...

Good morning, Jason. Thanks *again* for opening up for me.

No problem, Abby. You and Mark *deserve* an occasional morning together.

Sadly, I'm currently sharing my husband with the *IRS*. And by "*sharing*" I mean "*losing*."

They do get their cut of *everything*, don't they?

Oh, I pulled the *voice mail*. There were *lots* of messages for you from members of the Merchant Association about the *festival*.

Okay.

Oh, and we need *more message pads*.

I see that.

LATER...

Jason, this is *great!* This is going to be the best street fair *ever*.

You've done a stellar job with all this.

Now, do you want the *bad news?*

There's *bad* news?

You're going to have to meet with the town council for a *parade permit* and *exhibition permit*.

Placing the event on Jefferson Street will be good for *traffic*, but will irritate stores on the side streets. There's going to be *lots* of fights over position.

You're also going to need to rent a *ton* of equipment for the bands.

Remember when we used to *sell books?*

Oh, yeah. Good times.

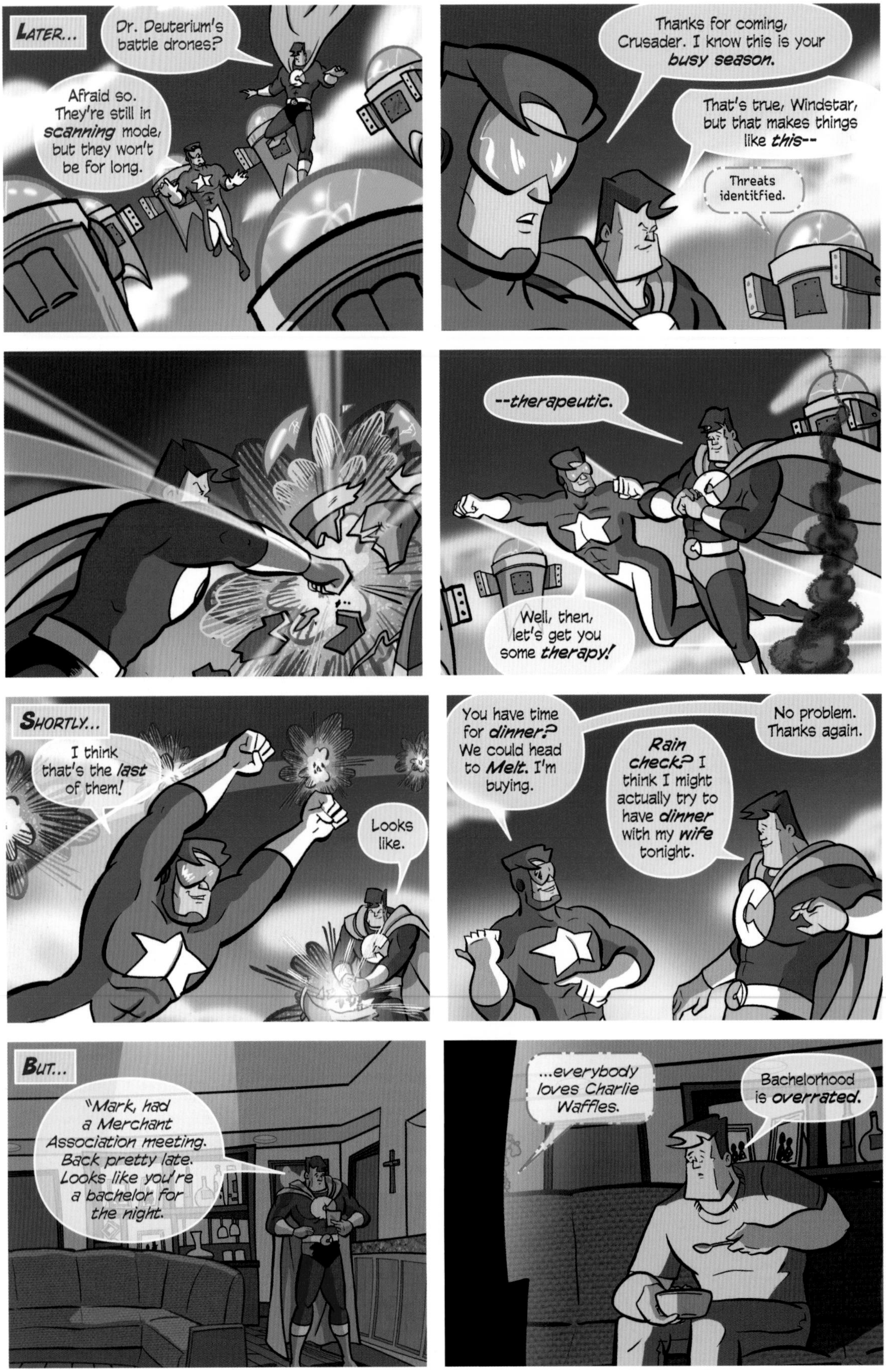
LATER...
Dr. Deuterium's battle drones?
Afraid so. They're still in scanning mode, but they won't be for long.
Thanks for coming, Crusader. I know this is your busy season.
That's true, Windstar, but that makes things like this--
Threats identitfied.
--therapeutic.
Well, then, let's get you some therapy!
SHORTLY...
I think that's the last of them!
Looks like.
You have time for dinner? We could head to Melt. I'm buying.
Rain check? I think I might actually try to have dinner with my wife tonight.
No problem. Thanks again.
BUT...
"Mark, had a Merchant Association meeting. Back pretty late. Looks like you're a bachelor for the night.
...everybody loves Charlie Waffles.
Bachelorhood is overrated.

PARIS...

C'est très bien de te voir, Amazonia!

Merci bien!

Hang back just a *little bit more*, Charlotte.

∃Sigh.∈ It seems *silly* to me. She's been to your store and your wedding. People *know* you two know each other.

True, but I'd rather them *not* know we're close enough to take a day trip to Paris.

She attracts her share of *paparazzi* and I'd prefer *not* to be in any *photos*.

It's just *safer* for Mark and his secret.

I suppose. She *does* draw a crowd. It's like being out with a *movie star*.

Except, of course, *she* doesn't need any security.

Ne me touché pas, crétin.

Mon dieu. Je suis vraiment désolé...

THE DRESS SHOP...

Mademoiselle Amazonia! *Welcome* to you and your friends!

Come, I have a *private salon* prepared and the *wine* is poured.

Merci, Daniel.

Fancy dresses, private rooms, *and* wine service? I could get used to this.

You're not hiring *personal assistants*, are you, Amazonia?

I don't know, Charlotte. I'd need a *reference* from your *current* employer.

Heh.

You know, on second thought, Paul would hate it if I didn't do something *arty* with my *art history degree*.

Good choice.

AND SO...

--wait, *what* do you mean you didn't do anything for your anniversary?

Charlotte, it's just the anniversary of our *first date*.

I've been busy with planning the *street fair*, and he's been wading through *Tax Hell*. We haven't had *any time*.

Besides, Mark and I have a *real* anniversary now, we don't need to celebrate the little one anymore.

Didn't you *save his life* on that first date?*

Yes, but that was *future* me, not past me. And it was actually *my* wedding day and her--

* In Love and Capes #12

Gah! How do you people talk about this stuff without popping an *embolism?*

Well, first we never do it without alcohol.

MANY DRESSES LATER...

I think this one's going to be the one.

Really? I'm not so sure.

What do you think?

Amazonia, that dress looks *great* on you.

And that's a *really* good color for you. *Definitely* go with that one.

I don't know--it just feels *strange*.

Oh, you've just never worn anything with a *collar* before.

AMAZONIA'S PARIS OFFICE...

I'll see you *next month*, Abby.

I *can't wait* to see you graduate.

Not as much as I can't wait to *actually graduate.*

The teleporter's ready when *you* are, Abby.

Amazonia, would you have *Paul call me* after you're done with this thing with his parents?

Sure.

'Bye!

Man, I have *got* to get one of those.

AMAZONIA'S HEADQUARTERS IN LIBERTY CITY...

You know, that was a *lot* of fun.

It *really was.* Thanks for inviting me.

Sorry to ambush you right as you arrive, Amazonia, but some *messages* piled up in your absence.

Let's see them, Grace.

See if you can push the Sephora meeting back to Wednesday, and tell the *Times* that, *yes*, we'll do an interview.

And I can call the *lawyers* back *after* I get Abby home.

Thank you.

You know, Abby, I love *having* a company. I just don't always like *running* a company.

You're *preaching to the choir* there, Zoe.

127

APRIL 15TH (TAX DAY)...

Today's the *big day*. How's Mark doing?

MOUSE in the HOUSE
the new book from M. FRANK BOKAUSEK

I'm not sure--

EARLIER...

Mark, do y--

Yikes!

WHOOSH!

Sorry. Super-speed.

Don't worry. My fault for opening the door.

--I've learned it's best to give him his *space* when he's working.

LATER...

--so now we have *no speaker* for the Women's Bureau dinner.

I know it's *short notice*, but could we convince you to *step in?*

I'd *love* to do it, Ellen.

You're a *lifesaver*, Abby.

See you *Thursday night*.

Did you hear that, Jason?

Yeah, it's a *big honor*. I'm just sorry you're losing your *only* night off this week. I hope you and Mark didn't have plans.

Oh, we'll be *fine*.

Besides, it'll be nice to be the one using the *"lifesaving"* excuse for once.

THAT NIGHT...

Hey, someone looks *relaxed.*

Most *definitely.*

So, our *long national nightmare* is over?

Yup. I e-filed the last return a *few minutes* ago.

Well, *congratulations!* I'm glad everything's done.

Were *our taxes* difficult this year?

Our taxes--?

Oh *no.*

YOU FORGOT OUR TAXES?

I was rushing around for my *clients*...and then there was this thing with the *Intellegizer--*

Mark, they have to be postmarked by *midnight.* That's in an hour and a half--

Okay, I can do this, right? Just another *crisis--*

Oh, we bought property this year. Why'd we have to do that?

There's mortgage interest and...

Mark?

Is there anything *I* can do?

Can you become a *CPA* in the next ten minutes?

Right, coffee it is.

LATER...

BEEP! BEEP! BEEP! BEEP! BEEP! BE

BEEP! BEEP! BEEP! BEEP! BEEP! BEEP! B

BEEP! BEEP! BEEP! BEEP! BEEP! B

What--?

Friction. Sorry.

FINALLY...

Abby, sweetheart, *wake up.* I need you to sign these.

Hmm? Wht tm izzit?

A little after one.

{Sigh.} Mark, you *could* have just filed an extension.

Don't worry, I have a *plan.*

You're not going *back in time* again, are you?

No. Well, *not exactly.*

11:25 P.M.

PACIFIC DAYLIGHT TIME.

Um... hello.

130

THEN...

RRRING! RRRING!

So, did we *make it?*

Postmarked before midnight. Everything's *good.*

Look, Mark, I've got an *early morning* so I'm *not* going to wait up.

I figured I'd let you know *before* you decided to do something sweet, like pick up a late-night sundae from *Ghirardelli's.*

Yeah, that *does* sound like the kind of thing I'd do, doesn't it?

A COUPLE OF DAYS LATER...

Mr. LaCroix--

--your parents are here.

Hello, son.

Thank you, Mrs. O'Lonergan.

Dad, Imani--

--I'd like to introduce you two to the *Princess Amazonia of Leandia.*

It's a *pleasure* to meet you, Princess.

I have to say, I'm a *huge fan.*

You *have* to tell me how you negotiated your deal with *Apple*.

Always with the *business*, this one.

Though I'm sure that *smile* of yours is quite a *negotiating weapon*.

You're *too kind*, Mr. LaCroix.

Sir, I brought some--

--snacks?

It's going a little better than I expected.

Clearly.

So...

Son, Amazonia was filling us in on the work her *foundation* does.

It sounds *wonderful*.

I was telling the story about that *surprise party* we threw for the kids last year.

Oh, yeah. They were *thrilled* to see some super heroes.

You know, we *used* to throw surprise birthday parties for Paul *all the time*.

Back when we *could*, of course.

Why *can't* they--?

Generally, it's *difficult* to sneak up on the *greatest deductive mind* of this *generation*.

THEN...

Paul, I have to say, I *really* like her.

Dad, I think that's the *first time* you've *ever* said that about *any* of my girlfriends.

Well, son, let's be honest. Sometimes you live the "*billionaire playboy*" thing a little *too* literally when it comes to choosing a ladyfriend.

Pretty? *Always*. Nice? *Often*. But not exactly *sharp*.

Wait, what about *Astrid*?

Yes. She was on *Celebrity Jeopardy!*

That *actress*?

Not as a *contestant*! She read a clue in the *Famous Frenchwomen* category.

It's closer than *you* ever got!

Say, did I tell you that *I'm* speaking at the *funeral* tomorrow?

They asked his *son*, but he said "*no*." I hear he *won't even be there* tomorrow. They had that falling out, remember?

No, you hadn't mentioned it.

Yeah, I...

Oh.

Dad, you know that'll *never* happen to us, right?

Well, you can understand my concern. I *did* arrange to have you kidnapped by warrior monks.

That's right. *Never mind*. You're on your own.

Dad, you do know I've never *resented* you for what you did, right?

Truly? Ever since you came back, I've always thought there was some *distance* between us.

Well, yes. But I've always felt *ashamed* that I was such a wreck that you had to call in the *big guns* the way you did.

I never realized. All this time, I've been ashamed that *I* wasn't a better father and that I *needed* to call in that help.

Really?

We don't need to *hug* now, do we?

No, *we're good.*

It looks like the boys are having a *moment* over there.

Well, it's *about damn time.*

Those two, they're the most stubborn, *taciturn* men I know. *Good* men, but they get in their own way sometimes.

I think Paul could use an equally *strong woman* in his life.

I think he's had one in his life for *years* now, Imani.

I'm going to *like* having you around.

134

LATER...

Hello?

Charlotte, it's Paul. Zoe told me to call you after *Operation: Meet the Parents* was over.

Oh, yeah. How'd that go?

Better than I could have hoped. They actually *got along*.

You're *kidding!*

I know, right? So, what was on *your* mind?

I need you to do a little bit of *sneaking* for me, if you don't mind. First, you'll need the *key* to--

Key? Please--

--you *forget* with whom you're speaking.

A COUPLE OF NIGHTS LATER...

Hey, look who's *home!*

Yeah. My *meeting* cancelled and--

Whoa! Look at all this! *Candles, wine...* and what's that I smell *cooking?*

Wait, this wasn't *you?*

No. And it wasn't *you* either? Then *who--?*

I don't know. I'm checking *now*.

It was *Charlotte.*

You think? Because I *thought* I picked up Paul's--

She just texted me. It was Charlotte.

135

She wrote: "*Married people actually spend time together. Don't make me do this again, doofus.*"

She's got a *point*.

Oh, *really?*

Not about the "*doofus*" thing, you doofus.

But we haven't had a lot of time together recently, have we?

You know, I bet you that I *never* really had a meeting tonight.

And it probably *wasn't* just a coincidence that I got rotated off *monitor duty* either.

We know some *great people.*

Yes, *we do.*

Still, I feel *bad* that we took each other for granted.

Don't. I think taking each other for granted is a *good* thing.

Excuse me?

I just mean, I spent the first couple months of our relationship living in *fear* that you'd *wise up* and start seeing someone who didn't disappear all the time.

I kind of like putting *my* hand out and knowing I'll find *yours* there.

Well, it's not like I don't appreciate knowing I have a *superhero* always watching out for me.

Still, maybe we should start making *Date Night* a thing?

Agreed.

Starting *right now.*

"*Charlotte, that was very sweet of you...*"

136

PARIS...

...but *what* made you think to arrange everything for them?

Well, I may not seem it sometimes, but I'm *very protective* of Mark and Abby's relationship.

"I'm single, and I'm *okay* with that, but still, I'd like to find someone for *myself* someday.

"I want what they have."

I've had *bad boyfriends* and *missed opportunities* and lousy luck so far.

"But when I see them together, I know that it's out there for me, too."

They're my *proof*--

"--that there really *can* be a happily ever after."

END

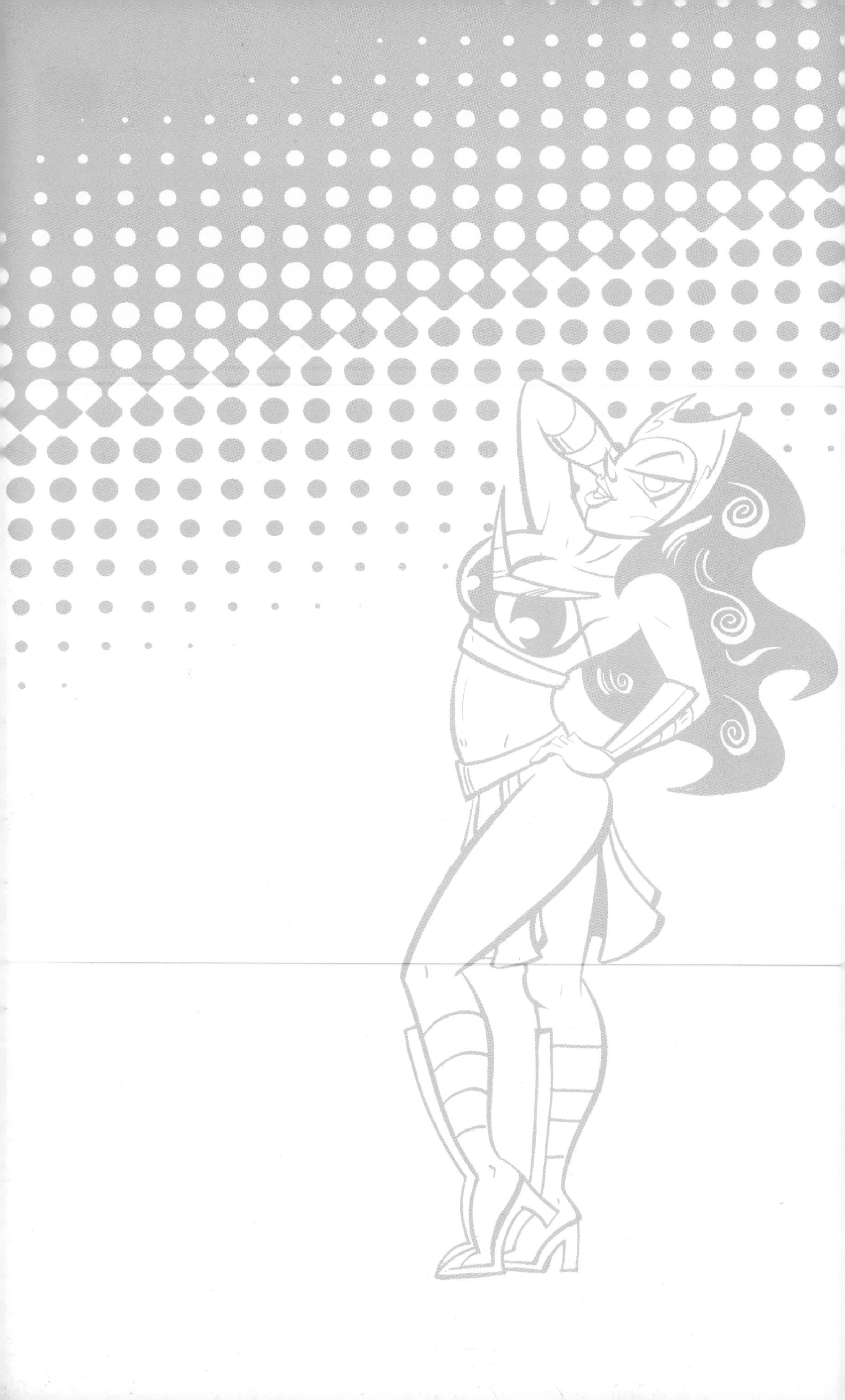

CHAPTER 6

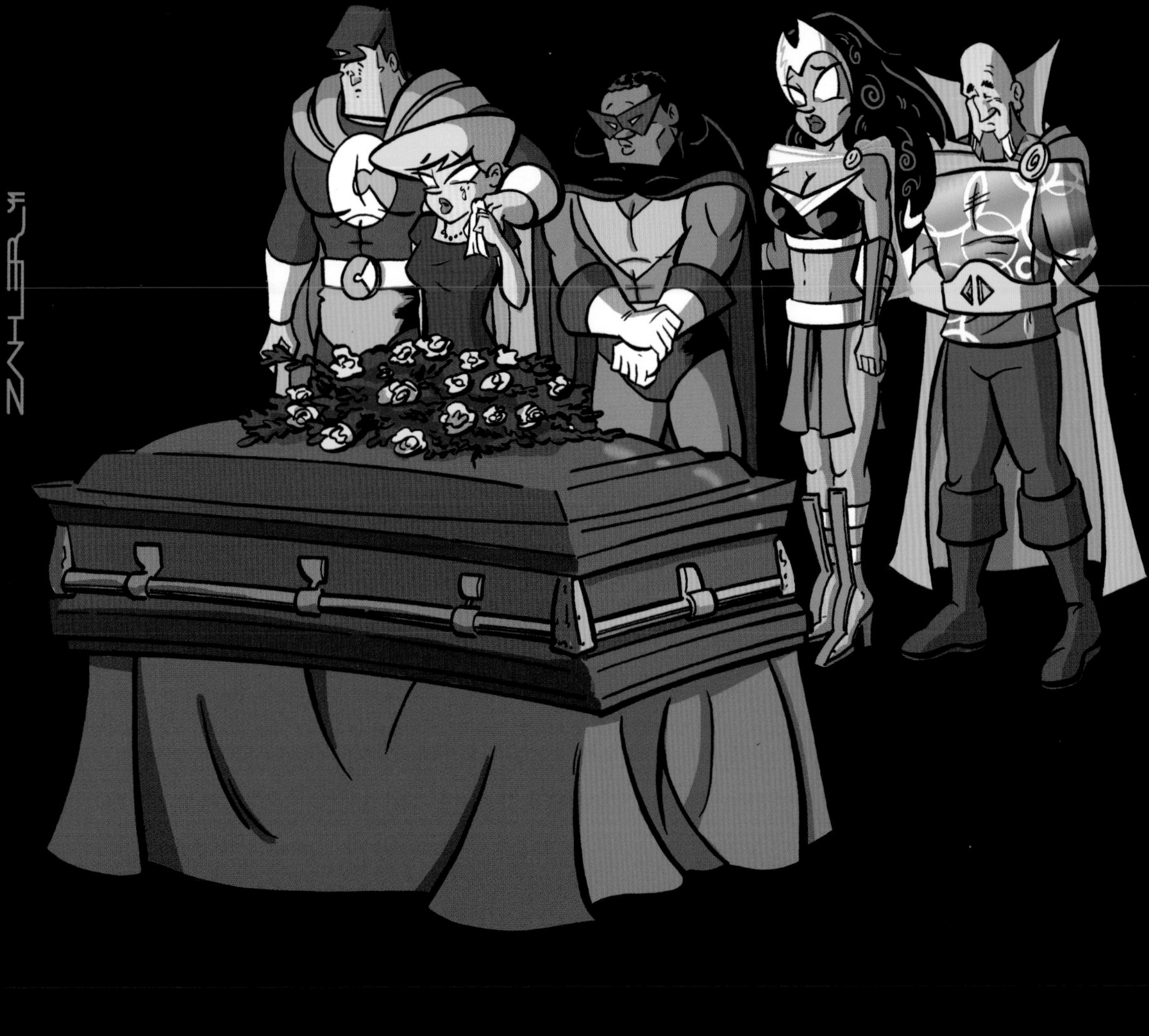

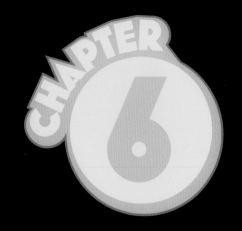

ALTERNATE COVER BY **STAN GOLDBERG & BOB SMITH**
COLORS BY THOM ZAHLER

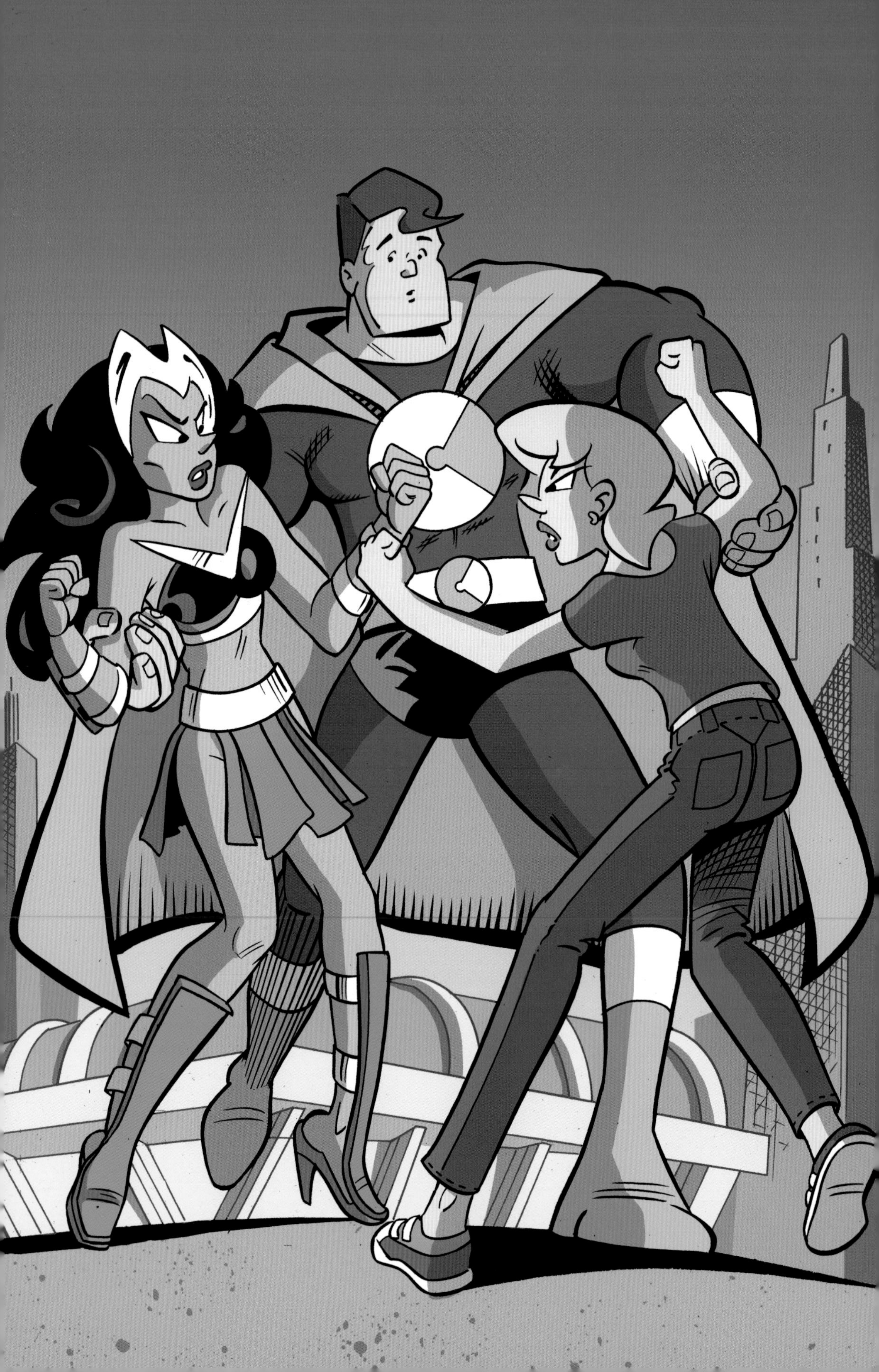

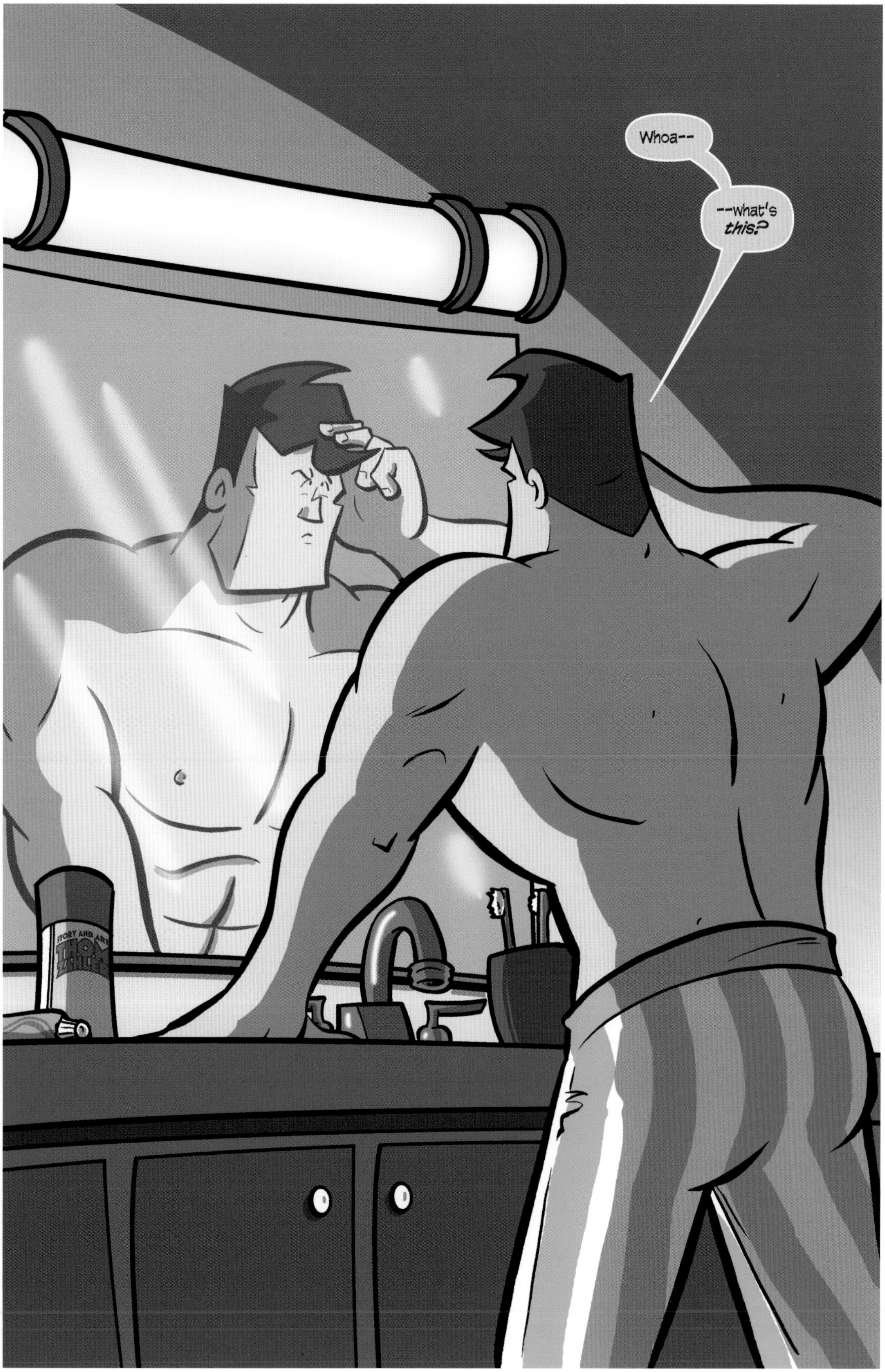
Whoa--
--what's *this?*
STORY AND

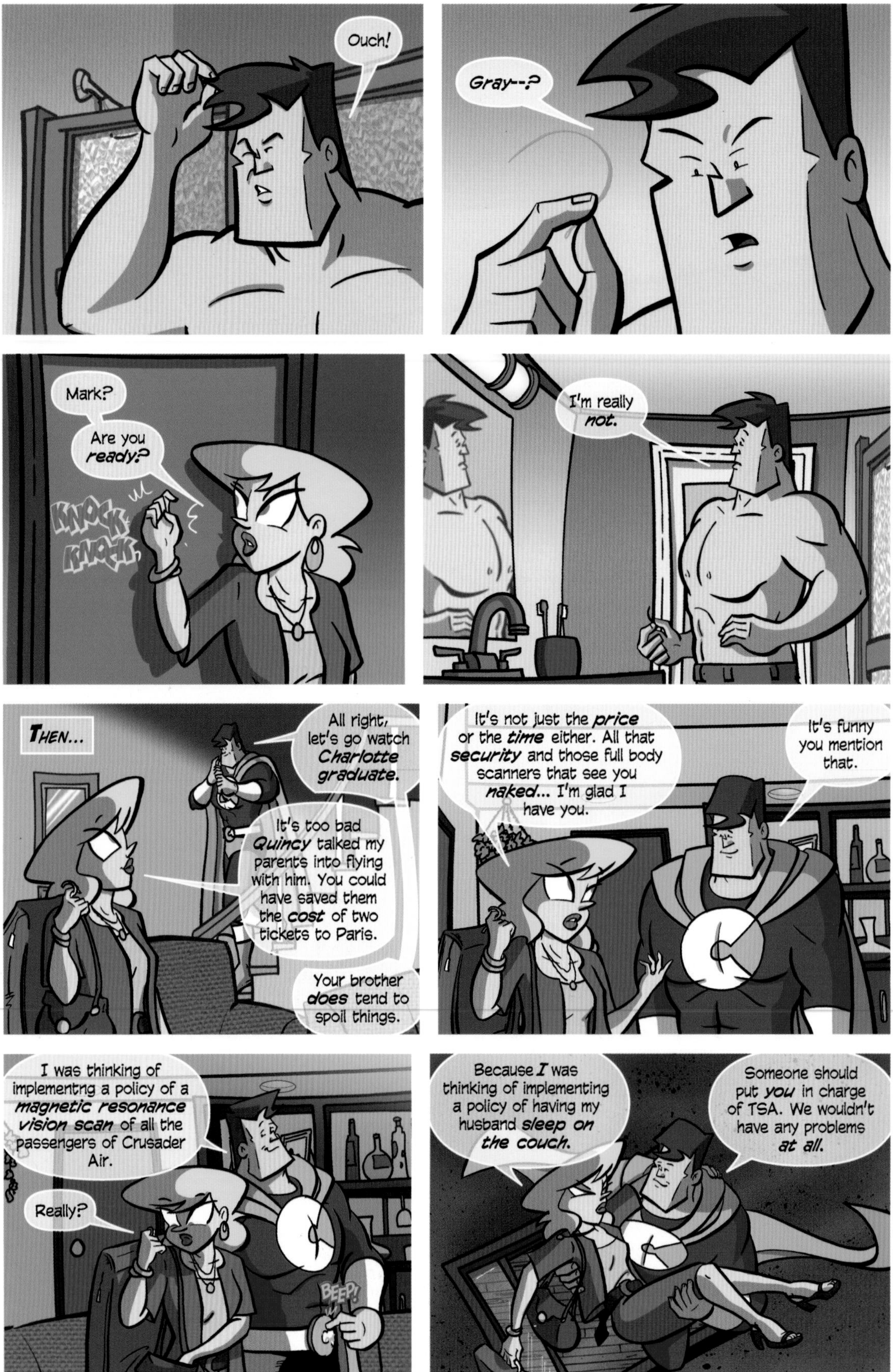
Ouch!
Gray--?
Mark?
Are you ready?
KNOCK KNOCK
I'm really not.
THEN...
All right, let's go watch Charlotte graduate.
It's too bad Quincy talked my parents into flying with him. You could have saved them the cost of two tickets to Paris.
Your brother does tend to spoil things.
It's not just the price or the time either. All that security and those full body scanners that see you naked... I'm glad I have you.
It's funny you mention that.
I was thinking of implementng a policy of a magnetic resonance vision scan of all the passengers of Crusader Air.
Really?
BEEP!
Because I was thinking of implementing a policy of having my husband sleep on the couch.
Someone should put you in charge of TSA. We wouldn't have any problems at all.

THE ÉCOLE DU LOUVRE AUDITORIUM...

Hello.

Hi, everyone.

So, Marky Mark, how was *first class?*

Tons of *leg room,* Quincy. It's the only way to travel.

Sorry we couldn't get on the same flight as you, though.

That's okay. Maybe we can see if there's something on your flight *back--*

Merci d'être venu, tout le monde.

Bienvenue à la *cérémonie de graduation* pour l'École du Louvre--

Wait, they're speaking *French?*

Um, we *are* in France.

Yeah, but I figured that just meant they'd all just talk like *Pepé Le Pew.*

THEN...

Félicitations, Mademoiselle Tennyson!

⇒Sigh!⇐

What *is* it, Quincy?

I had *fifty bucks* on Charlotte *not* graduating.

Abby, can you *believe* your brother?

What?

No. How'd he get away with *only fifty dollars?* I'm out a *hundred.*

That's what you two get for not having *faith* in your *sister.*

Now *pay up.* I need something to put in her *card.*

THE RECEPTION...

There she is!

Congratulations, Charlotte!

We're *so* proud of you.

And we're so happy you're finally coming *home*, too.

Guess what? I'm coming home to a *new job!* The Deco City Art Museum called back.

Uh, it starts as an *unpaid internship*, though, so, well...

You need your *old job* back, don't you? I'll have to talk that over with *Jason*.

I'd appreciate it.

I thought Jason told you he was looking to *cut his hours* this summer anyway.

He *did*. But you can't pass up having that kind of *deposit* in the *guilt bank*.

Sometimes you make me glad I'm an *only child*.

THEN...

Hey, Pipsqueak.

Hi, Quincy.

You know that, um, *I'm* proud of you, too.

I'm glad you went back and, you know, got your *degree*.

Yeah.

You are trying *so hard* to not ruin this moment, aren't you?

You have *no idea*.

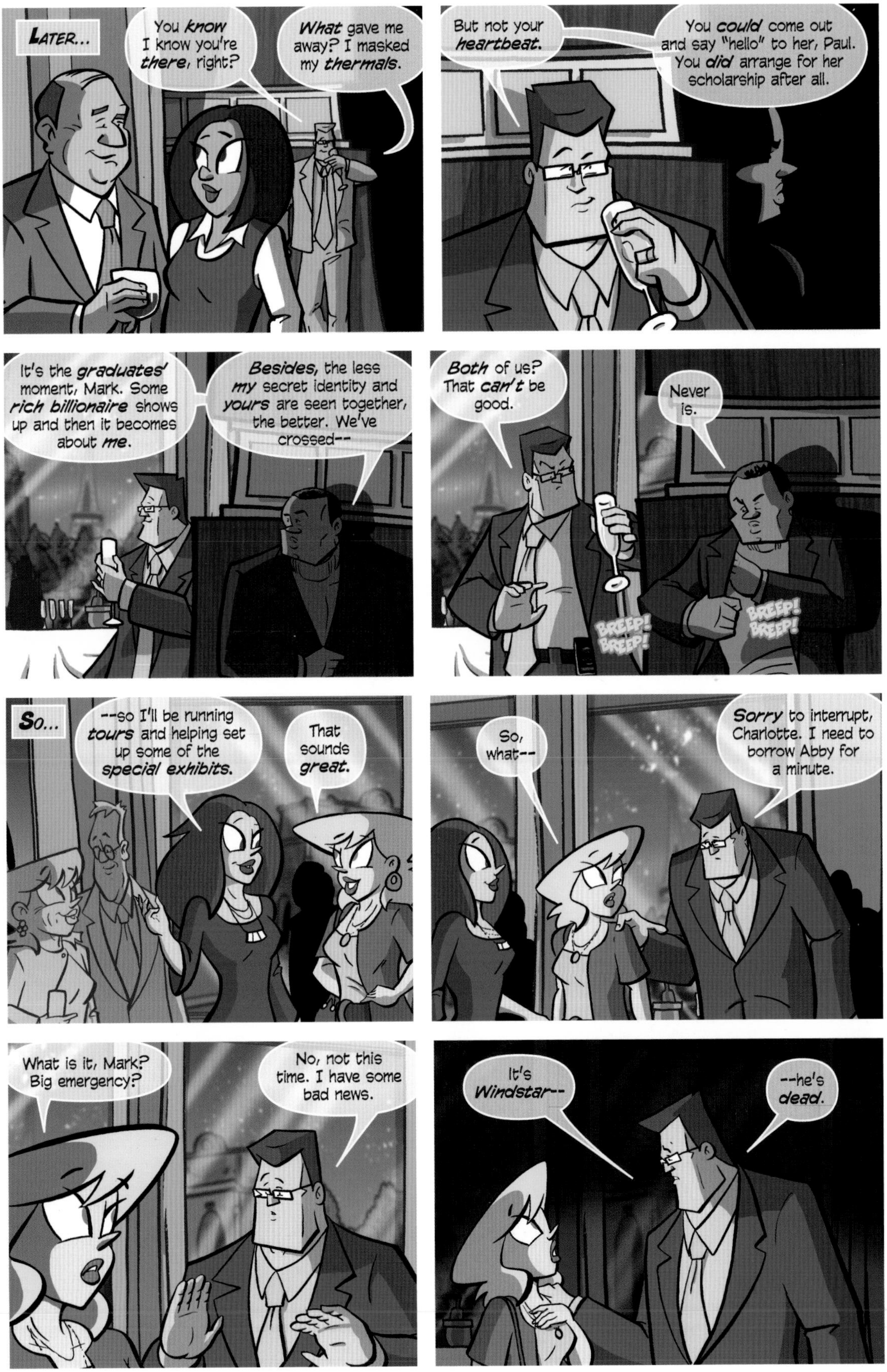
LATER...
You know I know you're there, right?
What gave me away? I masked my thermals.
But not your heartbeat.
You could come out and say "hello" to her, Paul. You did arrange for her scholarship after all.
It's the graduates' moment, Mark. Some rich billionaire shows up and then it becomes about me.
Besides, the less my secret identity and yours are seen together, the better. We've crossed--
Both of us? That can't be good.
Never is.
BREEP! BREEP!
BREEP! BREEP!
So...
--so I'll be running tours and helping set up some of the special exhibits.
That sounds great.
So, what--
Sorry to interrupt, Charlotte. I need to borrow Abby for a minute.
What is it, Mark? Big emergency?
No, not this time. I have some bad news.
It's Windstar--
--he's dead.

So, what happened?

It was *Quake Master*.

He'd been on a spree in Cleveland and weakened the *foundation* of some *hospital*. It started to *give* and Windstar--he *kept it up*.

But I thought he only had *flying* powers.

He managed to increase his *personal* antigravity field to encompass the *entire building*.

He kept it standing long enough for *everyone* to get out.

Everyone but *him*.

So, now, when we get back home, Paul and I have to report for *Miracle Max duty*.

Miracle Max?

You know, *Miracle Max* from *Princess Bride?* "Dead or mostly dead?" That's what *we* call it anyway.

We have to examine Windstar's *body*.

Examine it for *what?*

Well, in *our* line of work, death isn't always exactly *permanent*.

So a team of us make sure that it's *really* him, and that he's really *dead*.

I am *never* going to get used to knowing you, am I?

After being together for so long, I'm just glad I can *still* surprise you.

YEARS AGO...

--everyone in the League seems great.

And I can *already tell* that you and I are going to be *good friends*.

Not that I'm *denying* it, Windstar, but *what* makes you say that?

You still *smile* when you fly.

Everyone else takes it *for granted*. Golden Torch flew all her life, Doc Karma's *inscrutible*, and *Amazonia*, well--

--she acts like she's *entitled*.

HA HA HA HA!

What's so funny?

We used to *date*.

Got it.

You know, on my *Dad's* planet, *everyone* can fly. It's like walking.

But the first day I woke up above my bed, that was the *best day of my life*.

Did he *teach* you?

Yeah. I'm the *only one* in my family to develop powers, so it was a nice *father-son bonding thing* between us.

I'm a *little jealous*.

I had to figure my powers out on *my own*. Flight was the *worst*.

How did that go?

Took out my mom's favorite *buckeye tree*.

Don't tell *her*, though. She *still* thinks a *storm* brought it down.

CLEVELAND...

Gentlemen, I will leave you to your *somber duty.*

Thank you, Doctor.

CUYAHOGA COUNTY CORONER

All right, *Crusader,* you're up first.

Okay.

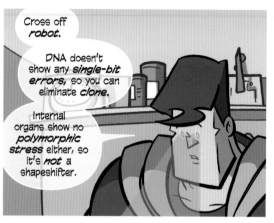

Cross off *robot.*

DNA doesn't show any *single-bit errors,* so you can eliminate *clone.*

Internal organs show no *polymorphic stress* either, so it's *not* a shapeshifter.

Alternate dimensional version?

No, residual radiation matches our universe.

Plus, you know, no telltale *goatee* or *gold lamé vest.*

THEN...

I'm perceiving no *magical influences* or *chronological anomalies.*

His passing seems to be purely in the purview of *science.*

I'm attempting to locate and contact his *spirit.*

Our friend is *no longer* on this plane. He appears to have moved past the *Great Veil.*

I am casting a *containment spell* so that his earthly vessel cannot be corrupted by opportunistic magicks.

So, he *won't* return as a *spirit of vengance?*

Once was *enough.*

Zounds! I returned that way but *once.*

148

MEANWHILE...

Hey, Jason.

Look who's stateside, the *conquering graduate.*

And *job stealer.* Abby fessed up that you're cutting *back* for the *summer semester?*

Yeah, I have to work on my *senior film.*

What's it going to be *about?*

I want to do kind of a *Romeo and Juliet* thing about two rival *winemaking* families and their *kids* who fall in love.

I've *even* got the title--

--Love and Grapes!

Jason, I--

Charlotte! I didn't hear you come in.

Both my employees--

Uh-oh.

What's *wrong,* Abby?

I just realized...now I'm *outnumbered.*

THAT NIGHT...

Hello, dear.

Hello, Mark.

How did everything go?

Well, it's *really* him and, as near as we can tell, he's really *gone.*

The League just had a meeting to plan things out.

And why do you smell like *gasoline?*

Oh, *sorry.* We had to wreck Mike's *car* to explain away his *civilian identity's* death.

The nice thing about being a superhero is that you've got *plenty* of places to channel the *"anger"* stage of *grief.*

Some of us who *aren't* famous without our masks are going to the *calling hours.* Would you like to come?

Absolutely, Mark.

I didn't know him as well as *you,* but he was *my friend,* too.

It's the *least* I can do.

Thanks.

You'll need to study *this,* then.

What is that?

Our *cover story.*

TWO YEARS AGO...

Hey, *Big Red.* Hold up a minute.

I heard you got *engaged.*

Just *last week,* in fact.

This is the *same* girl who was at your *ten-year party,* right?

Yeah. *Abby.*

I figured. I could *tell* she was one of the *good ones.*

How so?

She was *already taken.*

So, have you set a *date* yet?

Not yet. Abby's still checking on the *church.*

It's one of the things that work out so well with *us.*

With my power set, I've kind of become used to just *showing up* and figuring things out *on the fly.*

She, on the other hand, is definitely a *Type A master planner personality.*

So, basically, you're marrying a *female version* of *Paul.*

I may have to *call off* the wedding now.

In *that* case, can I get her number?

151

THE NEXT EVENING...

--I'm all for being *prepared*, but the whole cover story thing seems a little *extreme*.

I mean, he was our *real estate agent*.

That's true, but if someone asks how we *first* met him, we need to have our *story straight*.

And *we* have it easy. Blurstreak had to get *fake business cards* made up.

When you have a dual identity, you learn *very quickly* how to keep *secrets*.

And the *first* step is making sure you cover the *details*.

So, you're saying being a superhero has taught you how to *lie?*

Only *politicians* and *con men* do it better.

INSIDE...

--and that's Mike's *father*.

Wow, they look a *lot* alike, don't they?

Mr. Forrester, I'm *Mark Spencer*, and this is my wife, *Abby*.

We're *so sorry* for your loss.

How did you know my boy?

We were in the same ξahemξ *bowling league*.

I *under-stand*.

He was a *good man*, sir. One of the *best*.

Yes, he *was*.

That's *why* he's dead, isn't it?

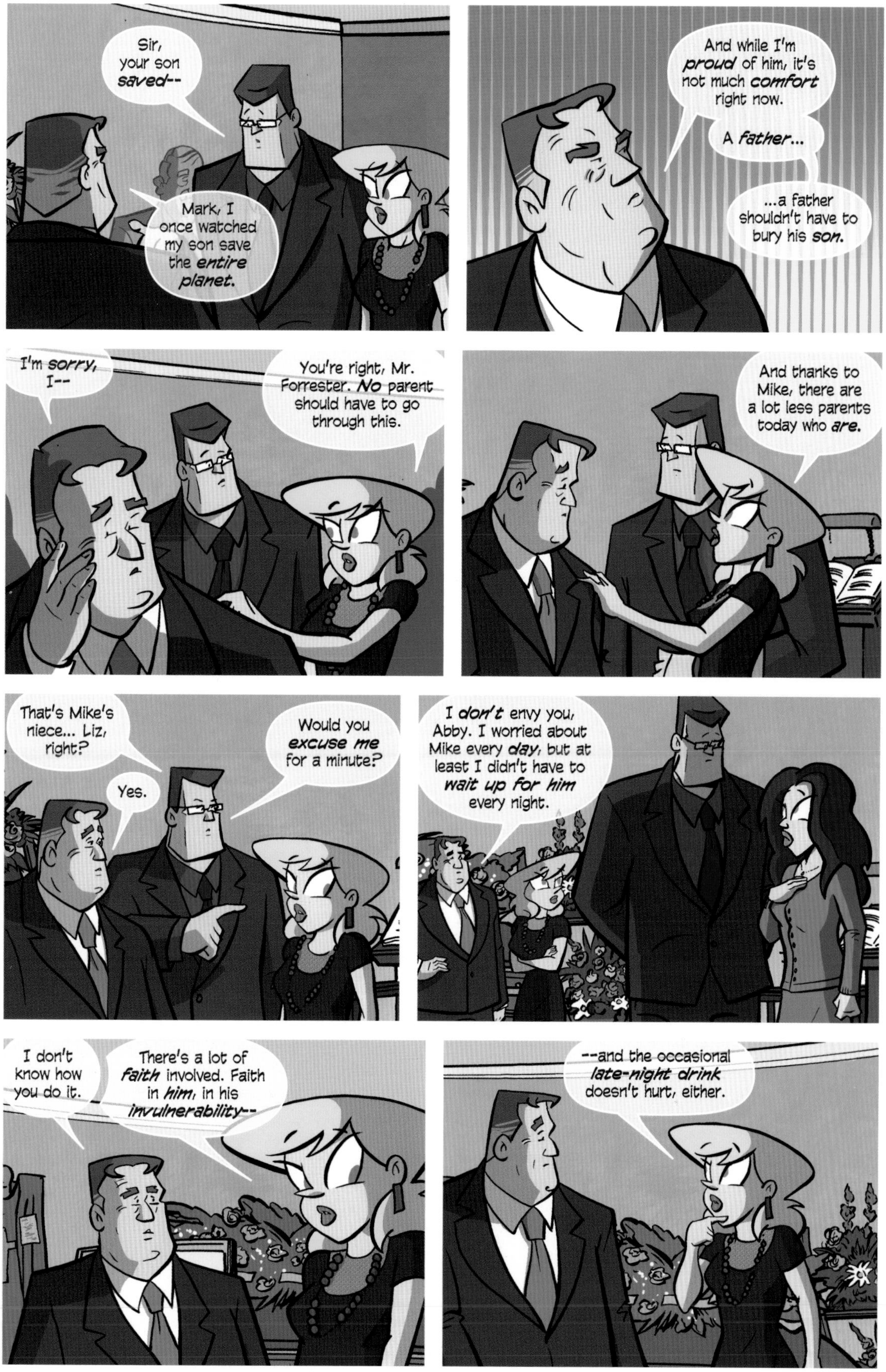

Sir, your son saved--
Mark, I once watched my son save the entire planet.
And while I'm proud of him, it's not much comfort right now.
A father...
...a father shouldn't have to bury his son.
I'm sorry, I--
You're right, Mr. Forrester. No parent should have to go through this.
And thanks to Mike, there are a lot less parents today who are.
That's Mike's niece... Liz, right?
Yes.
Would you excuse me for a minute?
I don't envy you, Abby. I worried about Mike every day, but at least I didn't have to wait up for him every night.
I don't know how you do it.
There's a lot of faith involved. Faith in him, in his invulnerability--
--and the occasional late-night drink doesn't hurt, either.

--so you're the *only other* member of your family with *powers?*

Yes. It skipped my *mother* and *Uncle Martin.* I didn't even have them myself until Uncle Mike *donated blood* when I had that operation last year.

We think that's what activated *mine.*

He was *so happy* when you got them. He *loved* flying and loved being able to share that with you.

He said you even *helped out* on a couple of missions?

Once or twice. He kept me out of the *spotlight.*

Is *that* what you wanted to talk about?

You want me to be the *new Windstar?*

The new--

Goodness, *no.*

Look, Windstar *isn't* a *mantle* or a *job description.* It was your uncle's *name.*

If you follow in Mike's footsteps, do it as your *own person* and because it's *your* choice.

Heroing's *not* an easy life, and *you're* still in college. Your grandfather never put on a costume, and there's nothing wrong with that.

But, if *you* ever decide to, the Liberty League and I are *ready to help.*

Here's my card. If you need *anything,* heroic or *mundane,* give me a call.

Also, the League is having a *memorial* for Mike. You, your grandfather, *anyone* who knows his secret and you want to invite, is welcome to come.

In there, they're celebrating your uncle's life. But it's only *half* his life.

Tomorrow, we're going to celebrate the *other half.*

MEANWHILE...

So, how did you know Mike?

He was my *husband's* friend.

Oh, I--

Mike was going to *Ohio Unversity* while *Mark* was attending Deco State.

They met at the OU/Deco State football game. Mark made some *Star Trek* joke and Mike got it. They kept in touch after that.

Then, after college, they played in the same *bowling league*, and...

Sorry. That was probably *more* than you needed to know, wasn't it?

Or wanted to.

Hey, I'm back.

How did it go?

Just *fine*. She's a good kid. I've got a feeling we'll be seeing *more* of her.

She'll be coming to the memorial, too.

That's nice.

So, are you ready to go?

Whenever you are.

Besides, I'd like to protect anyone else from another one of your *info dumps*.

Have I ever mentioned how much I *hate* your super hearing?

155

SIX YEARS AGO...

Excuse me. It's *Windstar*, right?

Eh?

I'm the *Crusader*. From Deco City.

Can I ask you a *question?*

I've heard there's someone around here *impersonating* me.

Have *you* seen anything?

Um, yeah... *about that.*

That was *me.*

Why would you pretend to be me?

Well, it's like this. A friend of mine invited me to a charity *costume party*. And it's just *reckless* to go as your *own* secret identity, right?

So I went as *you*.

Then these guys came in and pulled a *Hans Gruber*, holding hostages, trying to rob the place.

I couldn't get to *my* uniform, but I was dressed as you and I figured, "Hey, I can fly. Maybe that's *close enough*."

I used as many of my *flight powers* to fake some of *your* powers and took them down.

But you're *not invulnerable*, are you? And they had *guns?*

Yeah, but I told them shooting at me would only *add* an attempted murder charge and mostly make me *angry*.

Basically, I *bluffed.*

Hah! That's *great!* Wait until the *Liberty League* hears that one.

You know, we *are* looking for *new members*...

Really?

THE LIBERTY LEAGUE SATELLITE...

Amazonia, what are these memorials like?

We share *stories* about the deceased, comfort each other. And there's always a *closing speech* by one of us.

It's *my* turn in the rotation this time.

It's been a *League tradition* since before I joined.

It is. Though we've had to *modify* it over the years.

It's a *good* tradition.

How so?

Well, we've had to institute the *Doc Karma* rule.

Once you die *three times,* we impose a *ninety-day waiting period.*

So, it sounds like it's a lot like an *Irish wake.*

That's a good comparison.

On *Leandia,* we do something very similar. A little more *raucous,* of course.

For great warriors, the festivities can go on for a *week.*

We also show our *defiance* of death by engaging in the most *life-affirming activities* we can.

Life-affirming?

Let's just say Paul is going to *enjoy* it.

157

LATER...

Mr. Forrester, Liz, welcome to the satellite.

Thanks for having us.

It's our *honor*, really. Neither of you have been here before?

No, sir.

Well, feel free to take a look around.

Would you like anything to *drink?*

...

Liz, the Crusader asked you a *question*.

Don't worry about it, sir.

We lose a *lot* of people to that *view*.

It *is* quite a sight, isn't it?

Last time I saw Earth from *this* angle, my ship was plunging towards it at *terminal velocity*.

Still, it was the *best day of my life*. That was the day I met *my Melissa*, God rest her soul.

You know, I heard some people at the supermarket talking about *Windstar*.

Everyone knows he *died*, but no one seems to *believe it*. "Those guys 'die' like *soap opera characters*," I heard someone say.

Is he *really* dead, Mark?

I think so, sir. We have a list of things we look for when one of us dies. And we checked off *every item* we had.

Still, in all the years I've been doing this, that list has only gotten *longer*.

It seems like no one down there thinks it's *real*.

It's real *to me*.

THEN...

Everyone--

--it's time.

We come here today to celebrate the life of our friend, Michael Forrester... *Windstar*.

He stepped into the *skies* and chose a path as a *guardian of life*.

A path of *honor* and of *service*--

--and, as is too often the case, a *short* path.

He stood *bravely* against madmen and monsters, dangers and disasters--

--why once, I am told, he *even* dared to pull a *practical joke* on *Darkblade*.

Oscar Wilde said, "Man is least himself when he talks in his own person. Give him a *mask*, and he will tell you the *truth*."

If that is so, then *we* are fortunate. We had the honor of *truly* knowing our friend Michael.

So raise your glasses to a life *well-lived* and too-short. To our teammate, our hero, and our *friend*--

--to *Windstar*.

TO WINDSTAR!

To *my* son.

AFTERWARDS...

I think Mike would have appreciated that *send-off.*

Yeah, me, too.

I'm going to go change--

Mark, *wait.*

There's something I *need* to ask you. It's something I never thought of before.

But with *this* week...

Mark, can you *die?*

Can I die?

I mean, I know you're *invulnerable,* but what does that mean?

Well, *you* know better than me that I can be *killed.* You visited a timeline where the Evil Brain did just that.*

Though, as I understand it, he had to create a black hole *inside* of me to do it. That's a pretty *rarified event.*

* In Love and Capes #12.

But if you mean "Will I die like *everything else* does?"--

--I don't know.

My powers *didn't* come with an *instruction book.* I *don't know* what my future holds.

I do know I don't get *sick* and I *don't* get hurt--

--but I *am* getting older.

I found a *gray hair* the other day. I'm *still aging*... normally, I think.

But I don't know if my powers will keep me healthy *forever.* They might *fade* as I get older.

There's only one thing I *do* know for certain.

Whatever time I have, however *long* or *short*--

--I'm spending it with *you.*

That's *all* I need to know.

You know--

--if your powers *did* keep you from aging, I'd be okay being married to a guy in his *thirties* the rest of my life.

I appreciate the *sacrifices* you're willing to make.

It has *indeed.*

≥Sigh!≤ It's been a *rough week,* hasn't it?

You know, in the shadow of all this *death* and *mortality,* we need to do something--

--life affirming.

SIX MONTHS AGO...

Man, I'm gonna smell like a *chimney* for a *week*.

That's what you get for stopping a *forest fire*.

You stopped it. I just *evacuated* people.

True, but that let me *focus* on putting *out* the fire.

Some of the people I saved asked, "Why doesn't he just *blow it out?*"

What? That would have just *spread it*. You've got to make a *fire break*, and then pull in some water...

What *are* they teaching in schools these days?

I fear for the *next generation* of capes.

Well, this is *my stop*.

Thanks *again*, Windstar. *Sorry* you missed your volleyball game.

Hey, that's *the job*.

But we get to *fly* and *save people*. It's the *best* job in the world.

If I get to do this every day for the rest of my life, I'll *die happy*.

See ya.

A FEW WEEKS LATER...

Welcome back--

--Starlet.

Are you ready to become the League's first *junior* member?

Absolutely!

Let me show you around before everyone gets here.

I thought the Crusader said he was going to *be here.*

He *will.* He called in a couple minutes ago.

"He's running a little late."

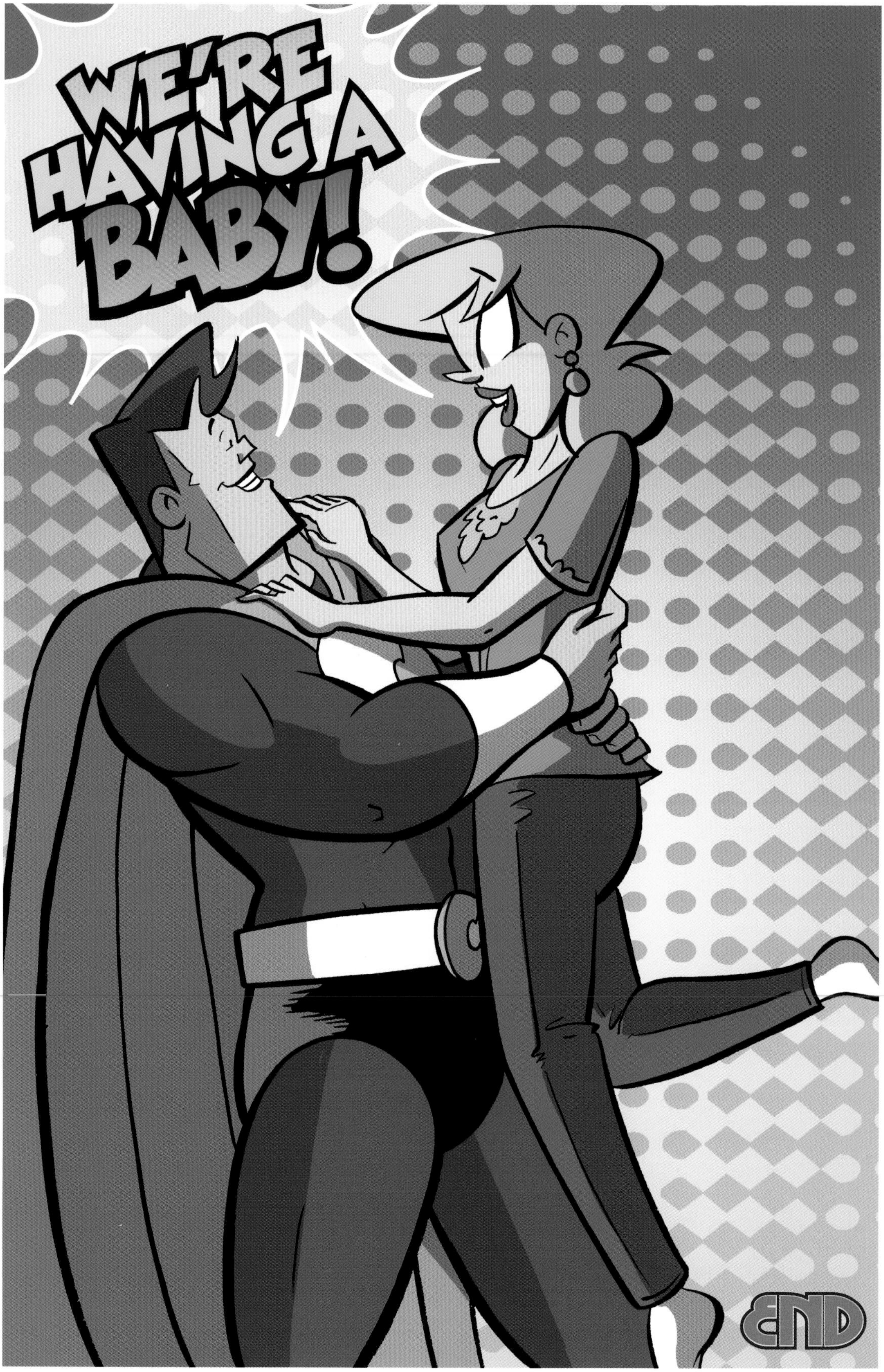
WE'RE HAVING A BABY!
END

BEHIND THE SCENES

JUST WHEN I THOUGHT I WAS OUT, THEY PULL ME BACK IN.

I'd applied to be part of 2010 Free Comic Book Day before even starting issue #12. As I finished up the wedding issue, the deadline for being told you were part of that event had passed. As I finished drawing Mark and Abby's flight into the sunset, I thought that'd be the last issue I'd draw for a while.

The day after I was told that I'd be part of FCBD, but even though the approval came through late, I was also told that the my deadlines weren't going to be altered. It meant that any break I thought I'd have was gone, and I'd have to start on *Love and Capes #13* immediately.

The problem, of course, was that I hadn't written it.

So, I had to follow up an ending that I thought was perfect, and I had to do it on the fly. A daunting task to be sure. I really didn't think I had it in me. And then I wrote the five funniest pages of *Love and Capes* I could remember.

I love the post-honeymoon scenes. Some people commented that we didn't actually get to see the honeymoon itself. That's intentional. Mark and Abby had a very normal week together. After everything I put them through in the first twelve issues, they deserved their one-week break.

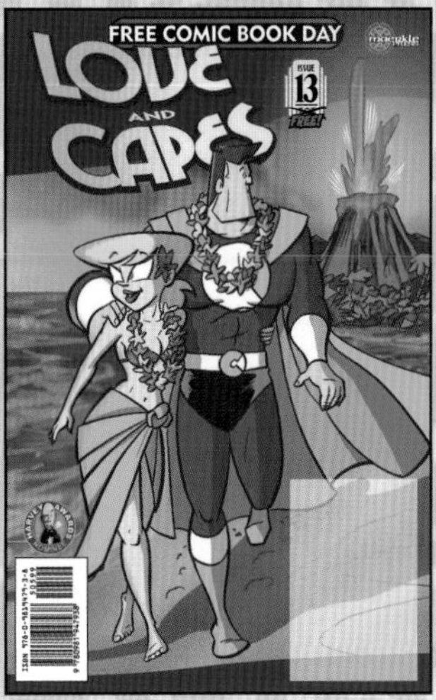
FREE COMIC BOOK DAY
LOVE AND CAPES
ISSUE 13

(I, however, wouldn't have one for months to come.)

I knew the thrust of this issue would be revealing who Darkblade chose at the end of the wedding issue. Would it be Charlotte or Amazonia? I'd long ago said that Darkblade would never date Amazonia because I hated that sitcom staple of people switching partners and being okay with it.

But they'd started becoming this couple. I couldn't stop from writing the scenes. Zoe was confiding in Paul. There was attraction between them. And they worked well together. So I decided to steer into the skid and get those two crazy kids together.

I even went all the way. One of my favorite sitcoms, *How I Met Your Mother*, had done the same thing with Robin having dated Ted and starting to date Barney. *HIMYM* is often on in my studio as I work. So, the show Mark is watching that spurs him to go talk to Paul is very clearly *HIMYM*, and from the scene where Ted tells Barney it's okay for him to date Robin.

I briefly toyed with the idea of changing the book at this point. The end scene is perfect for Mark and Abby to hand the baton to Paul and Zoe and let them take over the book. It'd still be *Love and Capes*, just a different love and a different cape.

Obviously, I decided not to do that. Mark and Abby had more story I wanted to tell.

CALIFORNIA'S THE PLACE YOU OUGHTTA BE...

My original plan for *Love and Capes'* third arc was that it was going to include the newlywed year and Abby getting pregnant, ending with the birth of their child. But I realized I had so much stuff to cover, and five issues of space. I broke it into two arcs. *Ever After* would end with Abby pregnant, and whatever else would happen would happen in another series.

This caused some growing pains. Charlotte suffered the most. I knew exactly what would happen after she graduated. But during? I didn't have a lot for that. And Paul and Zoe were taking up more room. So Charlotte, maybe my favorite character, got pushed to the side. She's only in one panel in this issue.

Then again, it gave me the space to invent Mrs. O'Lonergan who is probably my favorite new character. Her mildly abusive relationship with Paul (based in part on the Michael/Dr. Morris relationship from the cancelled-too-soon *Now and Again*) became a font of comedic gold.

I did some scenes of Mark and Zoe being awkward around each other that I thought were important. Working through it would make the new normal, well, normal.

The plan was always to have Mark and Abby move to a new place. Having them buy Abby's building was always in my head, but I wasn't sure that it'd be believable. It still might be a little too sitcom-ish, but I do like the idea that Abby and Mark could actually get the loan in their own right. Paul and Zoe are there as backup.

This issue marks the begin of the Zoe/Abby relationship. I loved the concept that Zoe didn't know any other successful relationships, so to make it work, she had to turn to Abby. I wanted to make it different than Paul and Mark's. Tea instead of coffee is the obvious one, but there's a clear student-teacher relationship instead of Paul and Mark's equal-to-equal.

You'll notice that Windstar makes the first of many appearances in this run. He's a character I created when I was thirteen. I've got tons of never-written stories for him. That gave me a lot of backstory that I could reference, making him feel like an actual character and not the red-shirted guy on the original *Star Trek*. Incidentally, he was always supposed to be a real estate agent (like my mother) so it was a great way to bring him into the story.

He'd shown up in issue #4 and #8 of the original run, and is mentioned in #12. But, if I was going to kill him off, I wanted him to appear in more than that last issue.

If I was gonna kill him, I was gonna make sure it **hurt**.

IT COULD HAVE BEEN WORSE

I COULD HAVE GIVEN HIM A BUG'S HEAD, OR TURNED HIM INTO A CAVEMAN, OR SOMETHING ELSE.

I love this cover. Anytime you get to make a go-go checks reference, you're having a good day.

This whole issue was my homage to those Silver Age Superman Red Kryptonite stories. I wanted to put Mark in a situation where his heroing brought him into conflict with his in-laws. I'd had a vague plan to have Mark targeted by a bad guy as his parents were meeting Abby's parents way back in issue #11. I couldn't make that fit, and I'm glad I saved it for here.

It also gave me the chance to expand Abby's parents' characters. They hadn't had much of a presence in the book up to now. They'd been around, but never with the impact of Mark's parents.

Abby's dad, who barely spoke in his first appearance, got most of the attention. A friend of mine has a daughter (my goddaughter, actually) and I've got to witness a lot of that father/daughter relationship. I thought it'd be interesting to see what happened when your daughter brings home a guy who actually is perfect.

I got lucky with that story, too, but in the most unlucky way possible. While working on this issue, the water heater in my house broke, leaking water into my living room. My Dad, lovingly referred to as MacGyverDad because he can fix darn near anything, came over and installed a new one for me. So now you know why Mark's water heater breaks.

That means I can write off my water heater as research, right? (Note to any IRS agents reading this section: I did not do that.)

I got to pay off the "you don't have to like what your significant other likes; you just can't **hate** it" storyline from the last issue, too, with Amazonia finally going to a Cavaliers/Mavericks basketball game. I'm not a big basketball fan, but it was the talk of the town as Mr. James hadn't yet announced that he was taking his talents to South Beach. It was also on my mind for similar reasons to the water heater, but that's all I should probably say about that.

I did get to throw in some *SportsNight* references in that scene too, and that's always fun. Man, I loved that show.

In the middle of this issue, I did Comic-Con in San Diego, then went to Los Angeles for a week, and then to Disney with my godchildren the week after, giving me a three-week break that, while I needed, also ate up a lot of time. The first page I came back to? The scene where the Time Winders shoot Mark. I went from drawing nothing to drawing four superheroes, a Viking, a dinosaur, a Terminator, and a hipster time-traveling street gang. That was a little bit of whiplash.

And look, Windstar appears again. That's not going to end well for him.

CHARLOTTE WILL NOT BE IGNORED

THE MONTHLY SCHEDULE LET ME TRY SOME STORIES I MIGHT NOT HAVE DONE OTHERWISE.
Charlotte hadn't appeared in much of the run at this point, and I decided that the story of hers that needed to be told was how Amazonia dealt with her friendship with Paul. I had to work to write the characters, not the way I felt. I think Charlotte's awesome and can't imagine anyone not liking her, but I had to write Amazonia doing just that.

Mark and Abby almost become supporting characters in this issue because of that. This story was inspired by my friend Dee mentioning her high school reunion. I started thinking "What would happen at Mark's? At Abby's?"

When I gave it some thought, I got to use two plotlines that I'd considered but never used. I'd always wanted to show Abby's frustration at having such a great guy, but not really being able to brag about it. I'd also considered a storyline where Mark and Abby's meet for the first time, and Mark is targeted by the Evil Brain, using the same genetic locking technology seen here. All those things came together in my superhero version of Gross Point Blank.

If you look in the background, you can see John Cusack's Martin Blank staring at a pen. Look at Charlotte in Paris, too, and see the Doctor and Amy Pond, apparently grabbing lunch at the Cafe du Mobius, named after the famed French cartoonist. Heck, Abby's ex-boyfriend is named "Ted" after the lead character on *How I Met Your Mother.* References abound!

But back to Paul, Zoe and Charlotte. I played Charlotte's relative absence into a story point, having had Paul pull back from hanging out with her so much. I got to focus on Paul's backstory a little more, which for a throwaway line in #3 has become a pretty nice origin. He was a celebrity train wreck until his father had those Irish monks knock some sense into him. It also gave me some great story reasons for Zoe not to completely trust Paul and Charlotte.

This book also features the funniest panel I've drawn. Mrs. O'Lonergan wearing the *Battlestar Galactica*-style jumpsuit and refueling the Airblade cracks me up. Every time.

Oh, and Abby's nickname? In high school, she loved potato skins. Ordered them everytime she went out to eat with her friends. So she had Mark take her to a TGIFriday's at the end of this issue. Seriously. Well, and then they went home and did something "life-affirming," if you know what I mean.

ADMIT IT, YOU'RE LAUGHING RIGHT NOW, AREN'T YOU?

ME, MY CAR, AND 185 MILES OF ROAD

THIS WAS MY SAM SEABORN MOMENT. There's a great scene in *The West Wing* where the President gives a speech about a tragedy that happened on a college campus. "The streets of Heaven are too full of angels," President Bartlett says. Later, one of his advisors compliments his speechwriter, Sam Seaborn, on that particular turn of phrase.

"Yeah," Sam says, "I wrote that in the car on the way over."

I wrote this issue as I was driving my new car back from the dealership. The dealership was in Pittsburgh, so I had some time to kill.

It was right before New Year's and the tax bill in Congress was a huge news story. I'd heard that it was a big problem for accountants, as it made it impossible for them to start. And Mark's an accountant. I was really lucky with that. When I split the third *Love and Capes* arc into two parts, this issue was the one that I didn't have anything planned for. My Post-It note said "Something funny happens here."

So, what I came up with was a story about what happens when you do it all? I'd already done a story in #5 that showed the sacrifices and toll that being a hero exacts on his personal life. Here, I wanted to show him succeeding, and as a result burning the candle at both ends. It helped that Abby is a type-A super-businesswoman, so I could put her in the same boat. So this issue would feature them **not** spending time together.

In another savant moment, the whole "Darkblade's parents meet Amazonia" story came about just because I wanted to make the estate tax joke. After I did it, one of my Secret Society of Super Reviewers told me he'd really like to see that meeting. And then my brain was off and running.

Paul's father was always supposed to like Amazonia because she was a businesswoman, playing against expectations. The original plotline featured Paul being jealous of his Dad's approval, but again, you've got to write the characters. Paul was a better person now and wouldn't feel that way, and that led me down a much more interesting and touching path, I think.

With one issue left, and knowing what that one would be about, I worked in a lot of the last story points. We see Mark and Abby's finished apartment. And Windstar makes one last appearance.

TOO CLOSE TO HOME

IT WOULD HAVE BEEN NICE TO HAVE A LITTLE LESS EXPERIENCE WITH THIS. I was at a funeral for a someone I'd gone to high school with. Many years after we graduated, he still volunteered at the school, and it seemed like the entire student body showed up. It took almost an hour and a half to make it through the line to see the family. As often happens, my mind wandered and I started thinking "What would this be like for superheroes? They'd want to go, but have to lie to get there."

In that line, I came up with the seed of this issue. It changed along the way, becoming far less funny that originally conceived. I realized that if I played Windstar's death for laughs, really embracing the whole "death is transient" notion in comics, then I'd be lessening any death that follows.

Also, right as I was starting this, I lost my Grandmother, my Aunt Alice, and my friend Dwayne McDuffie. Grandma refused to take free copies of my books, insisting on buying and then reading every one. Aunt Alice bought me a copy of *How To Draw Comics the Marvel Way* for my ninth Christmas, which was a huge influence in my life. She also gave me the information about tryouts for *Who Wants to Be a Millionaire?* which led to me being on the show and winning enough money to make a down payment on a house. And Dwayne was a good friend and a source of counsel. A couple months before, he'd spent two solid hours on the phone helping me through a script, and pushing me in the right direction.

So the funeral scenes were well-referenced.

WINDSTAR SKETCH, CIRCA 1992. CLEARLY I USED MY OWN PHYSIQUE AS REFERENCE.

Once I decided to kill a character, I had to decide who. Obviously, Mark and Abby were off the table. I was having such fun writing Darkblade and Amazonia that I couldn't get rid of either of them either. So, that left the rest of the Liberty League and any other heroes I'd created along the way.

Doc Karma was a possibility, but I dismissed him pretty quickly. When I was going to play the book for laughs, I was going to have the deceased reappear in the next issue and no one comment on it, because that's comics. When it wisely became more serious (and thanks to Tony Isabella for pointing me down that road) Doc Karma needed to stick around to help with Abby's pregnancy. So he was safe.

I wanted to kill someone who had some heft and had actually made an impact in the book. It could have been Major Might or the Arachnerd, but Windstar seemed a better choice to me. We hadn't seen much of him, but he seemed to be friendly with Mark in a way Might and the 'Nerd hadn't been.

Windstar was a character I created back in eighth grade who I'd tossed into a couple scenes of *Love and Capes*. Back then, I wanted to create a character whose power was flight. That eventually morphed into gravity powers. I had a huge series planned out for him. He'd be based in Cleveland, like I was, and be the area's first superhero. I imagined him in the DC Universe and wrote him that way.

SKETCH FROM ABOUT THE SAME TIME. AND WINDSTAR IS ROCKIN' THAT MULLET.

That imagined series gave Windstar a sense of history none of the other characters had. When Windstar pretends to be Crusader to thwart some terrorists, that was originally a Superman/Windstar moment. Windstar's father says he saw his son save the planet. That was a story about Earth almost being wiped out by terraforming aliens, and only Windstar's half-alien DNA allowed him to stop it. Windstar had a niece who got powers of her own, and that was an important piece of backstory. (My favorite comic book "meta" line is when Mark tells Liz that "Windstar isn't a mantle or a job description. It was your uncle's name." Not that I think that happens way too much in current comics, of course.)

So he had a history.

Still, I needed to make his history count. Every sixth issue of *Love and Capes* has been a "season finale," and every one was a flashback episode. *Love and Capes #6* flashed back to Mark and Zoe's relationship. *Love and Capes #12* flashed back to Mark and Abby's first date. So this issue would flash back to Crusader and Windstar being buddies.

The first scene was the most important, taking place right after Windstar joins the Liberty League. He tells Mark that he knows they'll be buddies because they both love to fly. It establishes a bond between them that's unique. I needed to make their relationship different that Crusader and Darkblade's.

It also gave me the structure of having every flashback taking place in the sky. I won't lie: Four pages without any difficult backgrounds made making my deadline a lot easier. Here's something to notice, too: While the flashbacks jump around through time *Lost*-style, the first one takes place in the morning, and each consecutive one gets later until Windstar flies off into the sunset.

The other major story point is, obviously, the pregnancy. I have to say that I'm very proud of Mark and Abby's discussion of his mortality. I haven't seen that in comics before, but I think it's a natural topic for a superhero and his wife to talk about.

A friend of mine says that the reason why this issue works so well is that it covers all the bases. It goes from happy celebrations (Charlotte's graduation) to sad ones (Windstar's funeral and memorial), and goes from death to life. The end result is one of the best things I've ever written.

True to form, I finished and said "Whew! I need a break! I'm done with *Love and Capes* for a while."

And then I started first page of the next issue.

LOVE AND CAPES

WRITTEN AND DRAWN BY THOMAS F. ZAHLER

Thom Zahler is a noted writer, artist, and giant noodle connoisseur. He wanders the backroads and badlands of America, attending comic book conventions and extolling the virtues of *Love and Capes*, which has been known to cause laughter, induce good feelings, and even cure baldness.*

Zahler trained at the legendary Kubert School, learning the mystical art of Cartooning as well as how to survive exclusively on a diet of Cap'n Crunch. Upon graduating, he began drawing silly things for fun and profit all across the country.

In his travels, he has worked for the NHL Guardian Project, Claypool Comics, the Rock and Roll Hall of Fame, the Baltimore Spelling Bee and countless other clients.

* By "cure baldness," we mean "do nothing at all."

SPECIAL THANKS TO:

AMY WOLFRAM, BILL WILLIAMS, DEITRI VILLARREAL, SEAN TIFFANY, PAUL D. STORRIE, SANDI SCHEIDERER, JILL A. SMITH, ROGER PRICE, PAUL MEROLLE, JESSE JACKSON, MIKE HORKAN, CHARLOTTE FULLERTON, CARIDAD FERRER, HARLAN & SUSAN ELLISON, AND MIKE BOKAUSEK

WWW.LOVEANDCAPES.COM
TWITTER: @LOVEANDCAPES • FIND US ON FACEBOOK